R.A. Williams Library
Florida Hospital College of Health Science
671 Winyah Drive
Orlando, FL 32803

The Kellogg Imperative

Richard J. B. Willis

John Harvey
Kellogg's Unique
Contribution to
Healthful Living

D1473987

WZ
100
.K29
KH
2003

Copyright © 2003
First published 2003

All rights reserved. No part of this publication
may be reproduced in any form without prior
permission from the publisher.

British Library Cataloguing in Publication Data.
A catalogue record for this book is available
from the British Library.

ISBN 1 899505 90 3

Published by
The Stanborough Press Limited
Alma Park, Grantham, England
Printed in England

The Kellogg Imperative

DF 2014

N.A. 2018-2019

Richard J. B. Willis

John Harvey
Kellogg's Unique
Contribution to
Healthful Living

Contents

Introduction

The world of John Harvey Kellogg MD
(1852-1943) may seem at first sight remote
from our hi-tech world of sophisticatedly
developed clinical medicine and specialised
health promotion. Such is not the case.

I became acquainted with the work of Kellogg while
researching 'health reform' as part of an MA programme
(Willis 1984). As a result of that research I was impressed
that much of what is now accepted in the theory and practice
of health promotion – and indicated as future trends – is
clearly stated and anticipated in Kellogg's writings. In
particular, dietary reform, the 'Healthy City' movement, and
lifestyle behaviour change. I have chosen to look more
closely at the first of these while also indicating the broad
scope of Kellogg's work, the practical success of which can be
seen in the documented health advantage of Seventh-day
Adventists.

Kellogg's observations will repay closer study in their
totality, especially when we consider the wide-ranging
implications of the wholistic approach to health promotion
currently adopted. The affinity Kellogg's concepts have with
our contemporary health philosophy is very striking and
should merit considerable acknowledgement at the present
time. The reasons for this have not been explored. Students
might argue, given his many advanced concepts, that his time
is still to come. Or it may be that the close association of
health and religion prevalent in Kellogg's day acts as a
deterrent to secular researchers. Renewed interest in both of
these areas may yet stimulate serious investigation.

I am indebted to the late Dr Hugh Dunton, former
Curator of the Ellen G. White Research Centre, Bracknell,
Berkshire; the Secretary of the Ellen G. White Estate,
Washington DC; and the Curator of the Heritage Centre,
Andrews University, Berrien Springs, Michigan, for their help,

unrestricted access to, and copies of archive materials pertaining to health reform in the nineteenth century. Thanks also to Professor Theo MacDonald who encouraged the writing of this book; dissertation supervisor Dr Sebastian Garman for his interest in the subject; Amy Munson-Barkshire for indirectly stimulating this research through her lectures on the wholistic health promotion emphasis in America; Judith Willis and Dawn Tompkins, without whose secretarial skills neither the original dissertation (Willis 1993) nor this present book would have been produced.

The Kellogg Imperative is dedicated to G. Martin Bell, Administrator, and past and present staff at the Roundelwood Health Enhancement Centre at Crieff, Scotland, who have continued the tradition and ethos of the Battle Creek Sanitarium; to Paul Hammond, General Manager, and Dr David Marshall, Editor, of The Stanborough Press, who along with their staff trace their commercial lineage to the Battle Creek Steam Press and continue to produce health promoting literature; to Cecil Perry, Chair of the Boards of both institutions, who has steadfastly supported and realised the vision in the United Kingdom and Republic of Ireland.

Of course, not all of Kellogg's ideas are with us today, nor should they be. The book is not intended to be one of unqualified praise. As might be expected, many people did not like Kellogg's ideas or him as a person and have been quite scathing in their attacks (Whorton 1982; Money 1985; Deutsch 1997).

The fact that Kellogg came to embrace pantheistic views – which he stubbornly refused to recant – led to his severance from the Seventh-day Adventist Church for approximately the latter third of his life and did nothing to endear him to many of his former colleagues. This book is not concerned with this aspect of his life, important though it is; it focuses on his contribution to health promotion as it emerges from the health reform movement of the nineteenth century and becomes an established speciality in today's health arena.

Whatever his shortcomings there are aspects of Kellogg's life worthy of note; so this book provides background information regarding Kellogg and his times from his own writings and those of his contemporaries and commentators in *The Search for Utopia*, and is followed by three sections documenting *The Man and His Influences, His Message*, and *The Media* through which his health message was promoted. *The Road to Wellville* serves as a postscript to these sections. The choice of title for the book reflects both Kellogg's approach to life and the manner in which he was often perceived. We shall see what imperative drove Dr Kellogg to formulate and realise his great ambitions, his religious beliefs, the source of his knowledge, and the tremendous need of his day.

The Search for Utopia

'The notion of utopian thinking has got what the Americans would call "a bum rap"! Somehow, the term has come to mean hopelessly idealistic, airy-fairy, "pie in the sky" thinking that ignores the "real" world. That is because we have misconstrued the role of utopian thinking. Good utopian thinking provides us with a beacon to light our way forward and a goal to strive to achieve; it also tells us what we would like the world to be like, as opposed to what we think it will be like' (Hancock 1992:22).

John Harvey Kellogg was born into a utopia-seeking age which influenced his medical practice and health reform concepts to a very great extent. If he had his head in the clouds Kellogg also had his feet firmly on the ground. He devised his own utopian thinking in the sense that Trevor Hancock defines the term. He had a beacon and a goal, he knew what kind of world he would like and was well aware of the kind of world in which he lived. Kellogg looked for, and found, a 'systematic and harmonious body of hygienic truths, free from patent errors, and consistent with the Bible and the principles of the Christian religion' (Kellogg 1890:iii). While we shall see that a high moral tone was characteristic of the age, we shall also find that Kellogg was a deeply religious man who considered health to be a part of Christian living, and man himself in need of restoration to God's ideal. To this end Kellogg states:

'The guidance of infinite wisdom is as much needed in the discerning between truth and error as in the evolution of new truths. Novelty is by no means a distinguishing characteristic of true principles, and the principle holds good as regards the truths of hygienic reform, as well as those of other reformatory movements. The greatest and most important reformatory movements of modern times have not been those which presented new facts and principles, but those which revived truths and principles long

forgotten, and which have led the way back to the
paths trodden by men of by-gone ages, before the
world had wandered so far from physical and moral
rectitude' (*ibid* iv).

Health reform was to be established as a way of life and not
as a duty:

'If we undertake to go about this thing in a willing
way, God will enlighten our minds, and he will lead us
into right ways; . . . I think that people years ago tried
to live out health reform from a sense of duty, and just
as soon as they would begin to backslide a little, they
would abandon it altogether,'

and, more strongly,

'As long as we undertake to do things from a sense of
duty, we will do . . . some stupid thing . . . , that will
upset everything, and entirely negative [sic] and
destroy all the good our obedience might do us'
(Kellogg 1897[1]:135).

In touch with the real world around him, Kellogg wrote, 'It is
high time that those who are seeking to reform the world,
should begin to preach the gospel of health. Instead of
sending missionaries to the Kaffirs, Hottentots, Kalmucks,
and Fiji Islanders, let us send a few messengers bearing the
glad tidings of good health to the great "unwashed", the
badly fed, the poorly slept, the generally neglected, and the
physically depraved multitudes of our great cities' (Kellogg
1893:v). Kellogg's concern for such persons was totally
genuine as is evidenced not only by his early recognition of
what are now regarded as 'inequalities in health', but also by
his own considerable charitable acts to remedy these
deficiencies, even through the residue of his estate after he
died.

Contemporary Opinion

There were many people who came to regard Kellogg as egotistical and even bombastic in his style – hence the *Imperative* of the title – but friend and foe alike could not disregard his all-consuming enthusiasm for his work as a medical practitioner, health writer and reformer, and his acknowledged inventive genius in medical equipment and health foods. Kellogg was also a sensitive man who disliked criticism and suffered intense periods of depression (Kellogg 1886). He was totally committed to the cause that he had espoused, with his health education, health promotion, health reform, 'biologic' or 'physiologic' living – call it what you will – absorbing every waking moment through a long and full life.

Kellogg has been variously described as 'the health educator *par excellence*' (Schwarz 1964:191), as one of the greatest health educators who ever lived (Schaefer 177:191), as being years ahead of his time (Brown n.d.:91), as deserving a Nobel Prize for his writing (Schwarz 1964:236), as one of the greatest individualists and leaders in medicine (GH.1944:14), and a distinguished international authority in the field of scientific labour (*ibid*). Dr William S. Sadler, who trained at Battle Creek, concluded that 'Dr Kellogg could do more things well than any other man he had ever known' (Schwarz 1964:44).

Brief Biography

John Harvey Kellogg was born in 1852 in Livingston County, Michigan, to Mary and John Preston Kellogg. One of sixteen children, John was born on the family farm in the Tyrone township. He moved with his family, devout Seventh-day Adventists, first to Jackson, Michigan, and a couple of years later to Battle Creek, Michigan, where his father started a broom factory. Years later J. H. Kellogg and his younger brother William 'Will' Keith Kellogg both put Battle Creek on the map through their work. *The Detroit Free Press*

described the brothers as 'teamed to bring the world to
Michigan and take Michigan to the world' (DFP. 1964:4B),
though they could not have had an inkling that this would be
so when they first arrived in Battle Creek.

J. H. Kellogg's youthful years were spent working in his
father's business. At the age of 12 Kellogg learned typesetting
– a significant turning point in his life – at the Battle Creek
Steam Press, owned and operated by Seventh-day Adventists.
At 14 he was a proof-reader; and at 16 a public school
teacher – in spite of his own inadequate schooling. He made
up for his educational deficiencies by extensive reading and
part-time study. When he was 17 he attended high school for
a year in order to graduate.

Reluctant Health Reformer

Kellogg wanted to be a teacher and had a particular interest
in chemistry. However, family friends and leaders in the
Seventh-day Adventist Church, James and Ellen White,
persuaded him to attend a medical course and helped to
provide the necessary financial assistance. Kellogg reluctantly
agreed and went first to hydropath Dr Russell Trall's Hygieo-
Therapeutic College in 1872. Somewhat disappointed by the
six-month medical course from which he graduated with an
MD, Kellogg made up some of the course's shortcomings by
class attendance at the University of Michigan at Ann Arbor,
and later graduated with a regular MD from the prestigious
Bellevue Hospital Medical School in New York.

In 1876 when Kellogg returned to Battle Creek he was
appointed – again reluctantly! – superintendent of the fairly
recently opened Western Health Reform Institute, located in
Battle Creek and operated by the Seventh-day Adventist
Church.

During his medical studies and while serving in his new
appointment – and for the rest of his life – Kellogg was also
the editor of the *Health Reformer* journal.

A New Start

Kellogg renamed the Institution and the journal. Showing his early commitment to the positive concept of health, he renamed the institute the 'Battle Creek Sanitarium', in the process adding the new word 'San*ita*rium' – conveying the idea of life and health as opposed to 'san*ato*rium', a place for the sick – to the English dictionary. The title of the journal was changed to *Good Health*. Commenting on the change of title in one of his editorials, Kellogg wrote, 'If we do not in this journal actually supply the precious boon [good health] itself, we hope to tell the way to find it, and once gained, hope to teach our patrons how to keep it' (GH 1879:20).

Kellogg received many 'accolades' as the Battle Creek Sanitarium underwent almost endless expansion and prosperity. The clientele were a virtual 'who's who' of America. The building itself became one of the largest buildings in America and had added to it a school of nursing, and incorporated the American Medical Missionary College, attended by many later prominent men and women, and was run on a non-sectarian basis but provided a number of denominations with medical missionaries.

The prestige of the sanitarium was further enhanced by the early adoption of up-to-date techniques as Kellogg continued his own education through extensive travel, mostly to Europe, and by his observation of and learning from the leading authorities of the day. George W. Reid says of Kellogg that 'he was an energetic builder, and under his leadership Battle Creek developed in the 1890s into the most famous medical centre in America' (Reid 1982:150).

Total Health

Kellogg's activities were not just confined to Battle Creek. He inspired others with his vision and involved himself in the realisation of his dreams. The writers of a *Health Education Journal* article, referring to the topical subject of 'healthy cities', says that one of the cities 'has defined its approach to health as "holistic" and "social". By "holistic" we mean that individual mental, physical and social well-being are considered to be interdependent. By "social" we mean that health is influenced by interacting social, environmental, economic and personal factors; that people's behaviour needs to be placed in its social context and individual and collective social responsibility for health acknowledged' (Halliday 1992:44).

Such was the nature of Kellogg's utopian thinking that he had already actively developed these concepts before the turn of the century. Kellogg worked with Jane Adams in the establishment of settlement houses in Chicago, helping to contribute to the emerging urban planning and social work professions in America (Spectrum 1990:37).

By pen, voice, and intense activity, Kellogg spent a lifetime seeking reform in the interacting areas of social, environmental, economic, personal factors and behaviours. When he died at the age of 91 he had lived long enough to see the reality of his utopia. Let us now see what influences shaped the man and enabled him to rise above others of his generation.

The Man and His Influences: A Merging Stream of Paradigms

General Influences

'Anti-medical propagandist of the 1920s, Anne Riley Hale, defined the essential creed of health reform as the belief "that the Kingdom of Health, like the Kingdom of Heaven, is within you" and is to be gained by hygienic righteousness' (Whorton 1982:4). Her observation would have met with agreement from health reformers. At the beginning of the nineteenth century a number of theories of disease were sweeping the north-east corner of America in what would emerge as a full blown health reform movement. The approach to health up to that time had centred around the religious beliefs of the various people who had emigrated to America to escape the religious persecution in Europe. Bryan W. Ball (1981) documents the extensive health teaching of the Puritan movement which left its indelible mark on the American colonies. These include: the concept of the whole man, temperance in eating and drinking, and vegetarianism. Ball quotes as an example the seventeenth-century writer Thomas Tryon:

> 'Now the sorts of food and drinks that breed best blood and finest spirits are herbs, fruits and various kinds of grains, also bread, and sundry sorts of excellent food made by different preparations of milk, and all dry food, out of which the sun hath exhaled the gross humidity, by which all sorts of pulses and grains become of a firmer substance. So likewise oil is an excellent thing in nature more sublime and pure than butter. And if you do eat fat flesh, let it be sparingly, and not without a good store of bread and herbs' (Ball 1981:176).

The Enlightenment and secular scientism had also reached and influenced these same places. Health reformers unconsciously bridged the gap between the paradigms. The resultant movement was characterised by its highly moralised pronouncements. The strong emphasis on spiritual perfection stressed in the religious revivals of the time and which dominated the age was translated into the need for a physical perfection. Horace Mann, prominent nineteenth-century educational reformer, was moved to write, 'If, in all things, the race should obey the physical laws of God, they would no more suffer physical pain, than they would suffer remorse, or moral pain, if in all they would obey the moral laws of God' (Reid 1982:25). This merging of the spiritual and the physical is continually to be found in the writings of health reform in the nineteenth century and persisted into the twentieth in, for example, Christian Science belief.

Medical Theories

On the scientific front, in addition to an increasing interest in vegetarianism, following a visit by William Metcalfe in 1817, of the Salford Bible Christian Church, Manchester (Antrobus 1997), and the leader of the UK vegetarian society, two main ideas came to prominence: the *Stimulation Theory*, and *'Heroic' practice*.

The *Stimulation* or *Brunonian Theory* (main advocate John Brown of Edinburgh, 1735-1788, who built on the ideas of Friedrich Hoffman, Halle, Germany, 1660-1742, and Boerhaave of Leiden, 1668-1738) proposed that health could be defined as an intermediate or optimum state of excitement. Over- or under-stimulation would cause or cure disease. Certain foods, drinks and health practices were said to contribute mostly to over-stimulation thus causing disease in the body. This state might be redressed by abstinence from the offending items or by the use of strengthening agents. These latter included opium, ether, wine, exercise, a flesh diet and spices. To weaken the over-stimulated body the physician would employ bloodletting, emetics, cathartics, fasting, rest, reducing the body temperature, and sweating (*ibid*).

'*Heroic*' practice, a fairly standard mode of treatment, consisted of a variety of active therapies intended to produce rapid changes in a patient. The fact that in the diseased state the person exhibits external evidences of his illness led to the belief that if these signs were reversed or changed the 'treatment' employed must be acting on the disease itself. Coincidentally, the agents used to bring about these changes approximated those used by the practitioners of the *stimulation* theory. Many of the treatments consisted of extremely potent agents for change and included strong poisons – obviously the more immediate and dramatic the change that took place, the more effective the treatment appeared.

Benjamin Rush (1745-1813), a signatory to the American Declaration of Independence and described as the dean of American physicians of his time, brought these similar practices together in his own regime of treatments. His national and foreign reputation made him one of the most influential men of his era and particularly influenced the orthodox medical professors a generation before John Harvey Kellogg (Reid 1982:29).

Residual Influences

There are evidences of the influence of the *stimulation* theory and the way that he responded to it in the writings of Kellogg:

> 'If by a stimulant we are to understand something which imparts force to the body when weakened by disease, then it is evident that alcohol can be of no service in this direction; for, as already shown, it is incapable of supplying force, undergoing no change in the body. All force arises from changes in matter. The forces manifested by the living system are the result of vital changes occurring in its tissues.

> 'If by a stimulant is meant something which excites nervous action, which calls out the manifestation of force, then alcohol is certainly a stimulant. And it is in this sense only that it is a stimulant. The lash is a

stimulant to a tired horse. It does not increase his
force, or make him any less tired. It only compels him
to use a little more of his already depleted strength.'
(Kellogg 1893:183, 184).

However, Kellogg's own concept of disease had matured
beyond those of the theories discussed. Writing in 1913, and
describing his own practice as *physiologic*, Kellogg decried
both of the prevalent theories by saying, 'Disease, then, is not
the chief object of attack in the physiologic method, but the
cause of disease. The physiologic method does not undertake
to cure disease, but patients' (Kellogg 1913:15). It does this,
he said, by restoring or normalising the vital forces (*ibid*).

The vital force theory that Kellogg continued to hold onto
was itself the product of a previous age, having come from
Paracelsus (1493-1541) via France and Sylvester Graham [see
page 22] into fairly common usage among the early health
reformers. The theory held that man was endowed from birth
with a vital force or stamina that attacked by disease,
responds in conflict. The vital force maintained at the
optimum level repels disease (Reid 1982:38). While the germ
theory and a more developed clinical approach to medicine
eclipsed the idea generally, recent times have seen renewed
interest in the concept as Dr Hans Selye, of the University of
Montreal, developed the theory in relation to stress and
changed the terminology in the process: 'Our reserves of
adaptation energy could be compared to an inherited fortune
from which we can make withdrawals; but there is no proof
that we can make additional deposits. We can squander our
adaptability recklessly, "burning the candle at both ends," or
we can learn to make this valuable resource last long, by
using it wisely and sparingly . . . ' (Selye 1974:28). Kellogg
seems not to have been influenced by the 'botanists' or the
homoeopaths who were also popular in some quarters.

Specific Influences

The specific influences affecting Kellogg can be traced to two distinct sources: those originating from Kellogg's instruction by the best of the orthodox practitioners of his day at Bellevue – although it must be borne in mind that even these eminent men held certain reform ideas and were involved in other radical movements – and the direct influence of health reformers.

'Orthodox Practitioners'

Of the first category of influences, Kellogg was indebted to a number of his tutors. Dr Austin Flint, Sen, president of the new American Medical Association, together with Dr Edward G. Janeway, both outstanding diagnosticians, gave Kellogg and others who could afford the fee a more personal tuition than the general student would have had. It was Flint who introduced Kellogg to the scientific application of water found in the treatment regime of Vincenz Priessnitz (1799-1851); Professor Edmund Randolph Peaslee taught Kellogg obstetrics and gynaecology; Dr Stephen Smith, later to found the American Public Health Association, taught aseptic surgery; Dr Lewis Sayre, New York chief public health official, taught vaccination and other aspects of public health. Each tutor was regarded as outstanding in his field.

Later orthodox influences are almost too numerous to mention, as Kellogg acquired skills in a wide range of subjects useful to his work. These unofficial 'tutors' include Dr J. Mortimer Granville, foremost nervous disorder specialist in Britain; Anton Billroth, famed for his treatment of skin disorders and cancer; Theodor Billroth, noted gastric surgeon; Dr Wilhelm Winternitz, an ardent advocate of the Priessnitz water treatments; Dr Gustaf Zander and T. J. Hartelius, pioneers in exercise therapy in Stockholm; Ivan Pavlov, noted for his psychological experiments; and Wilhelm Konrad Rontgen, pioneer in the field of X-ray. Many of these individuals became friends of Kellogg. It was Kellogg's use of what was then regarded as unorthodox treatments that conferred orthodoxy on them. Within twenty years all the treatments resulting from Kellogg's continuing education were established and respected practice (Schwarz 1970:35). Dr Kellogg frequently cited from the written works or experience of these men in his own voluminous writings, acknowledging that they had all been part of his ongoing medical education.

'Health Reformers'

It was only natural that Kellogg would also be influenced by the health reformers of his day. In many cases there were no orthodox practitioners at hand particularly in what were pioneer settlements when Kellogg was a boy. Even if there had been it would have been no indication of quality in treatment at a time when almost anyone could be awarded a medical diploma and a licence to practise. Quackery flourished. Orestes A. Brownson in a university address said:

> 'The age in which we live is the age of quackery. We are overrun with quackery, with quackery of every description. I refer not merely to quack medicines, which, though bad enough in all conscience, are by no means the worst or most deleterious species of quackery with which we are infested. We have quack economics, quack politics, quack law, quack learning, and quack divinity; quackery everywhere, and sometimes one, in a fit of despair or spleen, fancies nowhere anything but quackery.' (Reid 1982:35).

Eminent health educator Dr Mervyn G. Harding comments of the age that it was 'a time of great confusion and medical ignorance in which orthodox medicine and quackery worked side by side, each mixing a little bit of truth with plenty of unadulterated nonsense' (Coon 1993:12). So frontiersmen had little choice, if any, regarding treatments. Home treatments were not only popular but necessary and cheap. The health status of the day was deplorable, with the average age of death at 39.4 years (*ibid*:11). With medical treatment characterised as ' "the four Ps" – puke, purge, plaster, and poison' (*ibid*) – it is little wonder that information was largely gleaned from the popular health journals of the day. Such information if successful was widely shared, thus giving hope to other sufferers. Health reform found a receptive market for its ideas. The interest created was satisfied with a flurry of health reform literature. The years 1830-1850, called the 'Jacksonian Era' after the governing president, and described as the 'rise of the common man' (Craig 1991:35, Reid 1982:31), saw an increasing distrust of the elite, intellectuals and professionals. With its emphasis on taking personal responsibility for – among other things – health, the reformers found receptive and fertile minds. Health reform stressed prevention rather than cure.

The core teachings of the majority of the reformers included: diet reform, avoidance of stimulating drinks and tobacco, regular exercise, good use of water, electrotherapy, good ventilation and sanitation, and the use of herbal remedies. The reformers did not agree on every aspect of one another's theories, each preferring to believe that he was right and the originator of a particular concept.

Some reformers rose to greater prominence than others and exerted a far wider influence. These had a more direct bearing on the development of Kellogg's own views on health reform and include W. A. Alcott, Sylvester Graham, Horace Fletcher, and doctors known collectively as the 'hydropaths'.

William Alcott

Dr William A. Alcott (1798-1859), a cousin to the father of the Alcotts of writing fame, drank only water and milk, repudiated meat, fish and stimulants and lived mainly on vegetables. We do not find this so remarkable, given that many had similar ideas. His contribution was the formulation of various 'rules' to be observed in regard to the timing of meals and the quantity of permitted items to be served. Such was the public interest in the views that he so forcefully expressed that in February 1837 the American Physiological Society was formed with Alcott as the first president (Craig 1991:36). Alcott's influence can be seen in Kellogg's writings, particularly in the area of diet. However, while there might have been broad agreement on the part of health reformers with Alcott's dietary views, his supporters often held divergent views. Professor Edward Hitchcock, president of Amherst College, Massachusetts, where the reforms of Alcott and others carried great weight, condemned fats – with frying considered the worst form of cookery. Unlike many other reformers he allowed sugar and spices, disallowed by the stimulation theorists (*ibid*: 37).

Sylvester Graham

Of greater prominence even than William Alcott was Sylvester Graham (1794-1851), the youngest of seventeen children and with a background of ill-health which Whorton cynically describes as 'the first requirement for becoming a health reformer'! (Whorton 1982:302). Graham was a mature student when he enrolled at Amherst Academy, which featured the same reformed diet as the college. Influenced by the health milieu at Amherst and by reading two books: Paris' *Treatise on Diet* and Francois Broussais' *Treatise on Physiology*, Graham turned from ministry in the Presbyterian Church to be an itinerant temperance lecturer (Craig 1991:38). He was adamant that his acquired views were original. Nevertheless, Graham did carry forward health reform in the area of diet, but in many other respects he was a supporter of the *stimulant* theory. Naturally, Graham's diet was vegetarian and he was a founder member of the American Vegetarian Society in May 1850. In addition to the normal range of vegetable foods he emphasised the use of unrefined flours in bread making. His biscuits and breads although healthy in grain content were not very palatable. Writer Ralph Waldo Emerson labelled Graham 'the poet of bran bread and pumpkins' (*ibid*).

There is no doubt that Kellogg was influenced by

Graham's writings. He admitted as much on his graduation from Bellevue. Kellogg spent several weeks in postgraduate research in the Astor, Cooper and Free Medical libraries (Schwarz 1970:3), and later wrote home to a friend – W. C. White – 'I have found the same old "claim" that Sylvester Graham "worked" thirty years ago. I find that he left some very fine "nuggets" and I am gathering them up. I leave the smelting and coining until I get home' (Reid 1982:147). Unlike Graham, Kellogg was not a trained preacher as well as a health reformer and always felt diffident about the spiritual role he held as a leader of a Seventh-day Adventist institution. He confessed:

> 'I would give anything if only I had the spiritual force and strength which I ought to have. I am weak as a child in spiritual things, when I ought to be strong enough to inspire others. It seems to me that I can never be the man that is needed in the position which I occupy' (Kellogg 1886).

That is not to say that Kellogg did not speak, preach, or write on spiritual themes or that his mixture of the physical and spiritual was not as strong as Graham's – on the contrary. Notwithstanding, Sylvester Graham's efforts, to quote historian Richard M. Shryock, were ' "the spirit . . . of a sublimated puritanism" ', creating 'a sense of moral and physical salvation based on the model of theological deliverance' (Reid 1982:36). Indeed, Reid says of Graham that 'perhaps his most significant contribution to the health-reform movement was his binding the issues of health and morality into a single bundle, which provided the needed motivation to inspire action . . . his lectures involved the idea that reform fulfils God's desire that life should be of the highest possible quality and that reformers should enjoy their earthly pilgrimage' (*ibid* 42). Writer John B. Blake observes, 'What was new about Graham was turning health reform into a moral crusade' (Gaustad 1974:41), and, 'The aspect that gives the health reform movement its special flavour and meaning, was the evangelistic fervour of an era of moral reform. It made health reform a holy cause' (*ibid* 47). Whorton comments, 'The already well-advanced temperance movement was to a greater extent a microcosm of what health reform or "Grahamism" would become' (Whorton 1982:39). Whorton continues:

> 'Graham carried all that temperance baggage with him into health reform. He did, to be sure, reverse the temperance emphasis, giving much more attention to the physical effects of bad hygiene. But his heart was still dominated by moral anxiety, and his horror of spiritual sickness dictated his reasoning about physical health, pushing him to imagine the most dire bodily punishments for moral transgressions and to suppose moral rectitude must be essential for perfect health. As with teetotallers his hygienic temperance usually meant abstinence' (*ibid*).

Nor was it only alcohol that was linked to physical and spiritual perfection, as can be seen from a list of seven resolutions that Graham drew up:

'**Resolved**, That life, health, and all the physical interests of the human body are established upon precise and determinate principles, and that the highest welfare of man as an organic and animal being depends on the fulfilment of the constitutional laws of his nature.

Resolved, That a thorough knowledge of the anatomy and physiology of the human system is essential to the highest intellectual development; and that the greatest mental activity and power cannot be secured without a correct observance of physiological law.

Resolved, That the true principles of political economy are founded on the physiological laws of human nature and that the best interests of man in his social, civil and political capacities require that legislators and rulers should act with a just regard to those laws.

Resolved, That it is a duty morally binding upon man to study the principles of health, and to understand and obey those laws which God has established for the perpetuation of his existence.

Resolved, That the practice and advocacy of physiological reform is a duty which we owe to ourselves, to the community, to posterity, and to God – our Maker and Redeemer.

Resolved, That the highest moral and religious interests of man require a strict conformity in his dietetic and other voluntary habits to all the physiological laws of his nature.

Resolved, That the millennium, the near approach of which is by many so confidently predicted, can never reasonably be expected to arrive until those laws which God has implanted in the *physical* nature of many, are, equally with his moral laws, universally known and obeyed' (Whorton 1982:59).

It is in these resolutions that the significance of Graham's influence on Kellogg can be more easily seen. The last of these resolutions, concerning the anticipated millennium, in particular gave Graham his evangelical zeal and sense of urgency. It is unlikely that Kellogg would have disagreed with the content of any one of the seven resolves. Indeed, statements can be taken from Kellogg's writings which would indicate that he advanced these views wholeheartedly, and perhaps more clearly identified with their implications than any other person, including Sylvester Graham himself.

Edith Cole, writing in 1967 in the *Southern Speech Journal*, said of Sylvester Graham:

'We are witnessing today a resurgence of interest in the nutritional qualities of whole grain products and fresh vegetables. Wheat, rice and oat bran have swept into popularity again, and the problems connected with highly refined grains and cereals are well documented. While Sylvester Graham may have failed to establish a system of dietetics, he modified the old system to

include more fresh fruit, grains and unbolted wheat.
. . . Today, more than a century after his death, no
country is as concerned about its diet, physical
exercise, and health fads as America. . . . Graham is
remembered because a cracker bears his name; but his
writings and speaking in the 1830s and 1840s did
much to promote radical changes in diet, greater
exercise in fresh air and greater personal and corporate
cleanliness. The reforms initiated by Sylvester Graham
still have considerable influence on modern American
society' (Craig 1991:41).

That Graham's influence has survived is largely due to the
fact that Kellogg modified Graham's biscuits and breads (*ibid*
40), started a breakfast food industry and put nutrition on a
scientific foundation.

'Fletcherism'
Allied with the dietetic reforms of Graham was the
contribution of Horace Fletcher, described as 'a wealthy
merchant of Venice, Italy' (Kellogg 1912:1576), who
advocated the thorough mastication of food to increase its
food value. Kellogg seemed quite taken by him and often
referred to him. Indeed, Fletcher visited Kellogg at Battle
Creek in its heyday. Fletcher's experiments indicated that
there could be a two-thirds saving on food, with all that that
implies physically and economically, by thorough chewing.
While Kellogg was not in total agreement with Fletcher's
views, particularly in regard to discarding high fibre foods
because they could not be liquidised in the mouth, it was the
search for ways of assisting digestion that led him into the
cereal-breakfast-food industry that would later make him and
his brother 'Will' world famous. Kellogg felt that the
acquiring of the chewing habit early in life reduced the
individual's appeal for meat and condiments which Kellogg
omitted in his own dietary reforms (Schwarz 1970:47;
Whorton 1982:222). Nevertheless, Kellogg owed Fletcher a
debt of gratitude.

The Hydropaths

The Hydropaths on the other hand were less profound in their influence on Kellogg. Their main contribution was not the '*Heroic*' medicine that they practised, but, rather, the setting in which their treatments were performed. Prominent among the hydropaths were Doctors James Caleb Jackson, Russell Thacher Trall and Joel Shew. Each of these physicians headed water-cure institutions which, in their basic aspects, the newly-formed Seventh-day Adventist Church thought it worthwhile copying, initially for the use of its own ailing church members but then shortly for the community and beyond. Of the three physicians, Reid says that it was 'Trall's crusading spirit' that 'effectively transmitted itself to the Adventists, especially to Kellogg, and the health issue, which could well have remained an internal concern for Adventists, became an outgoing enterprise assuming the proportions of a moral and medical campaign' (Reid 1982:83).

It was Trall who laid emphasis on the scientific basis for vegetarianism which had hitherto been supported largely by moral and philosophic ideas. Although Trall decried the *stimulation* theory and moved in the direction of scientific nutrition, he still spoke with the strong moral overtones characteristic of the age: 'There is no delusion on earth so widespread as this, which confuses stimulation with nutrition. It is the very parent source of that awful . . . multitude of errors, which are leading the nations of the earth into all manner of riotous living, and urging them on in the road to swift destruction' (Whorton 1982:79).

Trall set up his water cure establishment in New York City in 1844 and it was only the second in the United States. It was devoted primarily to Priessnitzian baths and associated water treatments, diet, fresh air, good exercise, and an optimum amount of sleep. He went on to open other hydropathic institutions, including the Hygiean Home between Trenton and Philadelphia, and in New York his Hygieo-Therapeutic College where Kellogg became a student in 1872. Trall's influence extended beyond his own

institutions as he was also the editor of a number of journals
– the *Water Cure Journal* (1845-1861) which he took over
from Shew, and the *Hydropathic Review*, which he
transformed into the *Herald of Health*. Trall was a charter
member and office holder of the American Vegetarian Society
and even presided over 'a short-lived World Health
Association' (*ibid* 138, 139). Kellogg fell out with Trall, as
Trall would not accept chemistry as being useful to his
medical students and so Kellogg prematurely left the college.
Trall later mailed Kellogg his MD (Schwarz 1970:29).

The Western Health Reform Institute

About three years before Kellogg attended the Hygieo-
Therapeutic College, Trall had visited the Western Health
Reform Institute at Battle Creek and was pleased with what
he saw. He wrote in 1868, 'The Hygienic Institute at Battle
Creek . . . is in a prosperous condition. I wish this institution
abundant success, for it is practising the hygienic system in its
truth and purity, and will never, I am confident, compromise
its professed principles . . . for the sake of the almighty
dollar.' (Reid 1982:144). It was probably because of the
mutual feelings generated by visiting each other's institutions
that led the Whites to direct Kellogg to Trall's College where
his older half-brother, Merritt G. Kellogg (1832-1922), had
also attended.

Whorton, summarising Kellogg's later status and
commenting on his health promotion, said,

> 'Kellogg's head table was set at his Battle Creek
> Michigan Sanitarium, originally a Seventh-day
> Adventist institution designed to perpetuate Grahamite
> philosophy. Such, at least, was the sanitariums design
> in effect. In theory, though, Adventist health doctrine
> was free of any ties to the Jacksonian health reform
> movement. It was an independently acquired body of
> knowledge, not discovered by clumsy human probing
> but revealed by the Creator of the laws of hygiene

Himself. The Adventist "prophetess of health" was the
nascent church's spiritual director, Ellen White, a
woman who through most of her life experienced
visions' (Whorton 1982:201).

A Health Prophetess

It was this latter influence above all others to which Kellogg
repeatedly and gratefully returned throughout his life – the
writings and spiritual counsel of Ellen G. White (1827-1915).
She influenced his choice of profession, and her enunciation
of health principles and wise counsel guided Kellogg through
the years.

Ellen White's influence was no ordinary influence as she
was – and indeed is – regarded by Seventh-day Adventists as
a modern-day prophet. Seventh-day Adventism arose out of
the millennial expectations culminating in the preaching of
William Miller (1782-1849). This millennial expectation was
the spiritual counterpart of the physical reforms of the age
which included health reform (Whorton 1982:59). Ellen
White was an early supporter of the regrouped persons
disappointed by the non-fulfilment of Miller's claim that
Jesus would return on 22 October 1844. She served as an
unofficial leader and speaker and, more importantly to the
Adventists, as a prophet. Her writings were an account of the
visions that she received over a lifetime. A considerable
number of these visions related directly or indirectly to health
reform and administration. Unschooled because of an
accident at 14, she went on to write approximately eighty
books and around four thousand six hundred articles and
letters that helped to set the course of the Seventh-day
Adventist Church to the present time.

James and Ellen White were impressed that Kellogg should
be a doctor and helped to make it possible financially for him
to set out on a medical career. Reid wrote that 'John Harvey
Kellogg was the ideal man to lead the [Seventh-day Adventist
health reform] advance for his close association with the
Whites gave him authority in the church, his support of the

principles of health reform as taught by the church provided
contact for his efforts, and his regular medical training in one
of the nation's finest schools gave him a clear connection
with advancing scientific medicine' (Reid 1982:150).

Adventist health reform was not necessarily different in
every aspect from health reform generally promoted.
However, the source claimed for it was something new.
J. H. Waggoner, an early Adventist minister and writer, wrote
in 1866,

> 'We do not profess to be pioneers in the general
> principles of the health reform. The facts on which this
> movement is based have been elaborated, in great
> measure, by reformers, physicians, and writers on
> physiology and hygiene, and so may be found scattered
> through the land. But we do claim that by the method
> of God's choice it has been more clearly and
> powerfully unfolded, and is thereby producing an
> effect which we could not have looked for from any
> other means' (Craig 1991:41).

Dr James Caleb Jackson, noting the activity which this new
approach motivated, wrote to the editor of a magazine called
World's Crisis about Adventists, saying, 'They publish books
and tracts on the subject [health] arousing the attention of
their people, until really as a denomination, they are in
advance of any denomination of Christians in the United
States' (Reid 1982:110). The Adventist church now has
around four hundred and fifty hospitals, clinics and medical
launches besides four medical universities and other
paramedical training schools. An editor of the Adventist
Review and Herald magazine, introducing a new volume of
home health advice, said, 'The great subject of health reform
is getting to be well-defined and clear, by the light of which
all will be enabled to adjust their labours to their physical
capabilities, and thus have the surest guarantee against
breaking down and becoming inefficient in the future' (Reid
1982:92). The clarity which increasingly characterised the
Adventist health reform was due in no small part to the

visions Ellen White received. Some of the visions were for
the Church in general, others for specific individuals. Kellogg
was in no doubt but that the Lord had spoken to him
through Mrs White. He reiterated such thoughts right
through his life even after Mrs White was dead, and after he
had himself left the Adventist Church.

Speaking on one occasion to a conference of church
administrators and other delegates in 1897, Kellogg prefaced
his remarks thus: 'What I have to present to you consists of
words direct from the Lord himself. I believe that every
person here has faith and confidence that the words that I am
going to read to you are from the Lord; that they came from
divine impression; that they are the result of inspiration; that
they are instruction said to us, which we ought to receive'
(Kellogg 1897[2]:72). Kellogg expressed a growing
confidence in these divine revelations:

> 'It is impossible for any man who has not made a
> special study of medicine to appreciate the wonderful
> character of the instruction that has been received in
> these writings. It is wonderful, brethren, when you
> look back over the writings that were given us thirty
> years ago, and then perhaps the next day pick up a
> scientific journal and find some new discovery that the
> microscope has made, or that has been brought to light
> in the chemical laboratory – I say, it is perfectly
> wonderful how correctly they agree in fact.'

Kellogg went on to endorse a book that Ellen White had
written,

> 'Now in the preface to *Christian Temperance* you will
> find a statement which I presume not many of you
> have read. There is no name signed to the preface, but
> I wrote it. But if you will read it, you will find a
> statement to the effect that every single statement with
> reference to healthful living, and the general principles
> that underline the subject, has been verified by
> scientific discovery' (Kellogg 1897[3]:309).

Kellogg goes on, as Dr Mervyn Hardinge notes, to contrast

Ellen G. White's health teachings with contemporary health reformers:

'1. At the time the writings referred to first appeared, the subject of health was almost wholly ignored, not only by the people to whom it was addressed but by the world at large.

2. The few advocating the necessity of a reform in physical habits propagated in connection with the advocacy of genuine reformatory principles the most patent and in some instances disgusting errors.

3. Nowhere, and by no one, was there presented a systematic and harmonious body of hygienic truths, free from patent errors, and consistent with the Bible and the principles of the Christian religion.

Under these circumstances, the writings referred to made their appearance. The principles taught were not enforced by scientific authority, but were presented in a simple, straightforward manner by one who makes no pretence to scientific knowledge, but claims to write by the aid and authority of divine enlightenment' (Hardinge 2001:98, 99).

Kellogg found it difficult to understand why the work of health reform should not be taken up more fervently by church members, particularly as the injunctions were divine. He chided:

'You will be amazed; you will see what a flood of light was given us thirty years ago. There is, however, a more amazing thing than that, and it is that this light which was given to us at that time, confirmed as it is by scientific discovery – I say the most amazing thing of all is that we as a people have turned our backs upon this, and have not accepted it, and believed it as we should. I want to report it that there is not a single principle in relation to the healthful development of our bodies and minds that is advocated in these writings from Sister White, which I am not prepared to demonstrate conclusively from scientific evidence' (Kellogg 1897[3]:310).

Kellogg told the same group that the world was anxious to receive the knowledge that they could impart. He suggested that twelve sanitariums like Battle Creek could reach four to five thousand professional and prominent people each year who would use and further the information (Kellogg 1897[3]:312). He went further, 'If we would present ourselves to the world in the right condition in regard to these reforms we would not be a laughing stock, I assure you. We would be rosy-cheeked, bright-eyed, and more healthy. But instead of that, we present ourselves as an army of invalids'! (*ibid* 98).

James White had written in 1868 that 'People generally are slow to move, and hardly move at all. A few move cautiously and well, while others go too fast. The work of reform is not brought about in a single day' (White 1986:301). Kellogg returned to the theme of slowness in reform on many occasions. Part of the problem was the extreme position taken by some on health reform, not least by Dr Trall who had a regular column in the *Health Reformer*. For this reason, the editor of the *Review and Herald* stated in 1879 that 'Mrs White oftener feels called upon to speak upon the subject of health reform because of existing extremes of health reformers, than from any other reason' (*ibid*:305). Unfortunately, even by 1870 the *Health Reformer* was nearly extinct owing to cancelled subscriptions, the extreme views, and the illness of editorial staff (*ibid*:306)! Ellen White counselled, 'In reforms we would better come one step short of the mark than to go one step beyond it. And if there is error at all, let it be on the side next to the people' (*ibid*:307).

In 1938 just prior to his eighty-seventh birthday, Kellogg gave a lecture outlining the history of the Battle Creek Sanitarium. Speaking of his long-time association with Ellen White, Kellogg said, 'I found Mrs White a wise counsellor and a friend to whom I constantly appealed for advice which I followed to the best of my ability. I had the utmost confidence that the Lord was leading Mrs White's mind and I have the same confidence still. She was a godly woman who sought divine guidance and received it.' (Kellogg:1938).

Kellogg's confidence in Mrs White was confirmed in a little incident to which he alludes. Kellogg, while attending a conference, found himself in conversation with Dr Henry Hurd, then Medical Director of Johns Hopkins Hospital, Baltimore. Kellogg said later, 'He surprised, and I must confess, embarrassed me by saying, "Dr Kellogg deserves credit for having converted into a scientific institution an establishment founded on a vision" ' (*ibid*).

Hurd's statement would not have been contradicted by Kellogg. Shortly after taking over the Health Reform Institute and filling it with patients, Kellogg saw that the building would need to be enlarged. He wrote:

'I had so much confidence that the Lord would send us the building that I had allowed a picture of the one I had planned to be printed in the county history [a local newspaper]. After we had had two or three talks about the needs of more rooms for patients, the Elder [James White] told me one morning that the night before Mrs White had a remarkable dream. In her dream she saw that the little two-storey farmhouse with two small additions which had been made to it had grown in size to a huge building which extended clear down to Champion Street and that the fame of the institution had extended all over the world' (*ibid*).

'I do not for a moment doubt', he said, 'that kind Providence led Mrs White to recognise the principles on which the Battle Creek Sanitarium is based as divine truth and that this recognition was the motivating impulse which led J. N. Loughborough, Joseph Aldrich, my father and a few others to invest in the enterprise every dollar that they could spare from their scanty means' (*ibid*).

A Close Relationship

A filial relationship existed between Kellogg and Ellen White. He was able to say, 'I have always entertained the greatest respect and regard for Mrs White. Aside from my parents she was the best friend I ever had. She treated me as a son. As a young man I was a member of her family for months at a time' (*ibid*). In a letter dated 1886 Kellogg wrote tenderly to the widowed Ellen White ministering in Europe, 'I would as soon see my own mother lack for comforts as you. I have taken great pleasure in trying to make the last years of my mother's life the most pleasant and comfortable which she has experienced in her lifetime, and I assure you that anything in my power to do for you will be as pleasant and grateful a service as though it was done for my mother.' He thanked her also for her 'motherly regard', and in a postscript he and his wife said, 'We are both grateful to be called your children and to feel that you will extend to us a motherly care' (Kellogg 1886). In 1899 Kellogg wrote to Ellen White, 'I have loved and respected you as my own mother' (Numbers 1993:191).

Ellen White for her part felt free to speak frankly and kindly to Dr Kellogg. Concerned that he was greatly overworking, she wrote, 'Unload, unload, Dr Kellogg. Give that active brain of yours some period of rest else it will rest entirely, whether you choose it or not. I write to you as I would to my own sons' (White 1886). She also confirmed his leadership role by saying, 'You have been wonderfully successful in your career in doing a special work. God has raised you up as a man of opportunity to do this work' (*ibid*). Kellogg did not always feel up to this special work. He stated, 'You know I did not seek the place, and that I felt my unfitness for the position. It has always been a marvel to me that the Lord should have laid so great a burden upon so weak and deficient a person as I am' (Kellogg 1886).

Kellogg also had to deal with extreme views held by other reformers, including those in his own institution. He wrote:

'I have tried to be true to the interest of the institution and to the cause of health reform. When I became interested in the work, there were held and advocated many ultra and erroneous notion[s]. These I have tried to ferret out and to replace by correct views which might have the support of both science and common sense. Without denouncing the views of others which I thought to be ultra and extreme, I have tried to educate people in what I deemed to be better views' (*ibid*).

Acting as a mediator of divine principle and scientific view led Kellogg to comment, 'The position which I have held has made me a sort of an umpire as to what was true or correct and what was error in matters relating to hygienic reform, a responsibility which has often made me tremble, and which I have felt very keenly' (*ibid*).

How did Kellogg 'know' what was 'right' or 'wrong' in reform and avoid the quackery of his day? He posed this same question to a newly-graduated physician, Dr David Paulson, who was to join the staff at Battle Creek. Kellogg asked, 'Do you know how it is that the Battle Creek Sanitarium is able to keep five years ahead of the medical profession?' When Paulson said that he did not know, Kellogg elaborated:

'When a new thing is brought out in the medical work, I know from my knowledge of the Spirit of Prophecy [a term used to describe the prophetic writings of Ellen White] whether it belongs in our system or not. If it does, I instantly adopt it and advertise it while the rest of the doctors are slowly feeling their way, and when they finally adopt it, I have five years start of them. On the other hand, when the medical profession is swept off their feet by some new fad, if it does not fit the light we have received, I simply do not touch it. When the doctors finally discover their mistake, they wonder how it came that I did not get caught' (Staff. 1976:16,17).

That Kellogg 'did not get caught' was due in great measure to the quality of the revelations made to him. His belief that Ellen White was a prophet profoundly affected his work. His following of revelation was not out of a sense of indebtedness to the Whites or out of a misplaced gratitude. Nor was Ellen White a charismatic figure.

Talking to a group of people one day in the Battle Creek Tabernacle, he traced his attraction to Ellen White's writings to his typesetting days. Referring to her book *How To Live*, he said,

> 'I was about fourteen years of age then, and it was wonderful light to me. I appreciated it; it seemed to me the sweetest thing I ever heard, and I got hold of it and have tried to stick to it the best I could ever since. I owe my life to that fact. I should not be here today if I had not tried to follow that light and truth' (Kellogg 1905:83).

Referring also to the publication of the original book *Christian Temperance*, Kellogg stated, 'I set up type for that book. So it is no credit to me that I am a health reformer. It is my business' (Kellogg 1897[3]:310). It was the veracity of the words that Kellogg was drawn to – words that others have described as remarkable.

Independent Confirmation

Dr Clive M. McCay, renowned Professor of Nutrition at Cornell University in the 1950s, having none of Kellogg's connections to the White family or Seventh-day Adventists, also felt the force of Ellen White's writings. Following an interview with McCay, *Review and Herald* editor Francis D. Nichol wrote in 1959,

> ' "How do you explain that fact that Mrs White, with very little formal education and no special training in nutrition, so accurately set forth nutrition principles that are only now scientifically established?" He ruled out as wholly unsatisfactory the answer sometimes casually given: "Mrs White simply borrowed her ideas

from others." He observed that such an answer simply raises another question: "How would Mrs White know which ideas to borrow and which to reject out of the bewildering array of theories and health teachings current in the nineteenth century?" ' (Nichol 1959:4).

In the same article McCay observes,

'Every modern specialist in nutrition whose life is dedicated to human welfare must be impressed . . . by the writings and leadership of Ellen G. White . . . her basic concepts about the relation between diet and health have been verified to an unusual degree by scientific advances of the past decades . . . . In spite of the fact that the works of Mrs White were written long before the advent of modern scientific nutrition, no better over-all guide is available today' (*ibid* 8).

The Right Route
While Kellogg acknowledged his indebtedness to the health reformers of the past to a greater or a lesser extent, he was quite sure that the reforms advocated by Ellen White through the Adventist Church were the ones to follow. Recognising the virtual end of the old-style health reform movement, Kellogg wrote to the White's son, Willie,

'Trall's usefulness is almost ended, for money reasons. Hall is a make believe reformer. O. I. Fowler is a quack, phrenologist, and a renegade. Jackson is a humbug, and good old Dr Graham is dead. Our people [Adventists] are the only ones who have this reform on a right basis, and if anybody does anything, we must be the ones to do it' (Reid 1982:147, 148).

A century after the founding of the Battle Creek Sanitarium, the Seventh-day Adventist Church operated three hundred and fifty-four similar institutions around the world, employing over thirty thousand professional and service personnel, dealing with well over five million patients annually (*ibid* 146). Historian Gerald Carson made the observation that what gave Battle Creek its special flavour was the 'religious-health-medical doctrine of the Seventh-day Adventists' (Craig 1992:5). The influence spread beyond Battle Creek. Horace B. Powell, Will Keith Kellogg's biographer, comments, 'The Seventh-day Adventists with their tenets of the simple restorative methods of nature, and the use of hydrotherapy and vegetarianism – have made an indelible mark upon our country' (Powell 1956:52). We shall now see what tenets made this profound impression.

The Message:
Battle Creek and Beyond

Establishing 'Orthodoxy'

A contemporary of Kellogg, Thomas A. Edison (1847-1931), perceptively wrote, 'The doctor of the future will give no medication, but will interest his patients in the care of the human frame, in diet, and in the cause and prevention of disease' (Werbach 1986:179). The aptness of this description to Kellogg and his biologic living is striking. Such an individual might well have been regarded as an oddity in the nineteenth century.

Whorton, while grudgingly describing Kellogg as 'a competent surgeon', placed him in the oddity league – 'his [Kellogg's] distrust of drugs and advocacy of "natural" methods relegated him to fringe status in the eyes of the most orthodox practitioners' (Whorton 1982:203). The statement is far from accurate. In fact Kellogg was more likely to have practised sounder medicine than many of the so-called orthodox, if a statement by the president of the Massachusetts Medical Society in 1858 is anything to go by:

> 'The cumbrous fabric now called therapeutic science is, in a great measure, built up on the imperfect testimony of credulous, hasty, prejudiced, or incompetent witnesses . . . . The enormous polypharmacy of modern times is an excrescence on science, unsupported by any evidence of necessity of fitness, and of which the more complicated formulas are so arbitrary and useless, that, if by any chance they should be forgotten, not one in a hundred of them would ever be reinvented' (Werbach 1986:16).

Well aware of this state of affairs, Kellogg, James White, and others involved in the running of the Western Health Reform Institute, agreed that,

> 'if they were to continue to criticise the practice of physicians of the day, they must be able to bring to the discussion of their points of difference a storehouse of

scientific knowledge of chemistry, anatomy and
physiology. They must be able to keep abreast of the
important medical discoveries that were being made at
the time' (Schwarz 1964:25).

Schwarz also points out that contrary to the practice of
earlier health reformers 'Kellogg did not attack and discredit
the medical profession. He set their conversion as his goal'
(Schwarz 1970:35).

The Michigan State Medical Association, guests of the
institution in 1877, found everything to be entirely regular
and rational (Robinson 1943:215). Through the pages of the
Health Reformer (June 1877) Kellogg stated:

> 'We have no quarrel with the regular profession and
> there is no reason why we should be upon any other
> than the most friendly terms with those who are doing
> nearly all that is being done to conserve the public
> health, . . . It is the grossest injustice to charge the
> medical profession in general with such grievous
> crimes as total apathy to human suffering, . . . The
> regular profession embodies all there is of real science
> in the healing art. . . . Instead of constantly stirring
> up strife, and belabouring the profession in an
> antagonistic manner, let us take a conciliatory course.
> By this means we shall be enabled to disarm the
> prejudice of our medical friends, and thus secure their
> influence in our favour rather than against us' (Kellogg
> 1877[2]).

Kellogg's conciliatory approach was met halfway by a
change in attitude on the part of the orthodox practitioners.
Dr Ira Remsen, professor of chemistry at Johns Hopkins
University, said in an address given in 1879 to the medical
and surgical faculties,

> 'The tendency of the present generation of physicians
> is, I think, to rely less and less upon the action of
> drugs and chemicals, and to pay more and more
> attention to the circumstances surrounding the patient,
> so the discovery of purely remedial agents is becoming

day by day of less importance, and the accurate study
of those substances which we all necessarily make use
of – air, water, food in its various forms – is becoming
the great problem in medicine' (Robinson 1943:217).

The quotation regarding Kellogg's attitude to the medical
profession and the enlightened attitude of a considerable
number of important practitioners places into context an
incident that occurred to Kellogg in 1886. Doctors William
J. and Mina Fairfield, a couple previously employed at the
battle Creek Sanitarium, preferred charges against Kellogg at
the Calhoun County Medical Society. Kellogg wrote to Ellen
White in Europe:

> 'He did not undertake to attack my professional ability
> or honour, or my standing as a gentleman in his main
> charge, but attacked what he supposed was my most
> vulnerable point. He charged that I am guilty of
> writing books that are calculated to cause the people
> to have less confidence in doctors and drugs than they
> are accustomed to have . . . . The final verdict in the
> society was, "charges not sustained."
> . . . When it came to the final vote, himself and his
> wife were the only physicians out of nine of those
> present from the city of Battle Creek who voted
> against me' (Kellogg 1886).

The rest of the letter makes it clear that the stated reasons
were only a cover for personal malice. It seems the Fairfields
had been trying to get patients of their own for a rival
institution. Ellen White and others were well aware of the
real situation (White n.d.:14). Whorton's statement about
Kellogg's 'oddity', like Fairfield's charges, cannot therefore be
sustained.

Kellogg served on the US President's Committee of One
Hundred and served a number of terms on the Michigan
State Board of Health. In her proposal for one of his six-year
terms, Dr Beverly Harrison, secretary of the State Board of
Registration in Medicine, said of Kellogg, 'He is probably the

best-qualified medical man in the state for appointment on the State Board of Health. He not only has a national reputation as an expert in preventive medicine but an international' (Schwarz 1970:226). The following six months after his appointment saw the introduction of a travelling railroad health exhibit, health meetings for farmers' institutes, weekly health-press bulletins, the formation of a state health-education committee, and the authorisation of state public-health inspectors (*ibid*). Kellogg's wide interests, his unflagging enthusiasm, and his ability to be successful in the various ventures which he undertook singled him out as a new kind of doctor, making an art of preventive medicine.

Lifestyle Diseases

'The art of medicine', said Rene Dubos (1901-1982), 'involves the ability to select, intuitively as it were, those aspects of the total medical situation in all its complexity which can be manipulated not only by scientific medical technologies but also by any other kind of influence which promises to be useful' (Werbach 1986:118). Kellogg's regimen was an outworking of Dubos' definition. Given a choice, Kellogg would have stood by the old adage 'prevention is better than cure'. He would have preferred to see a lifestyle change in an individual. Despite his sterling efforts it is only now that preventive medicine is coming into its own.

Dr Kenneth H. Cooper, quoting from the *Journal of the American Medical Association*, states, 'In the coming decades, the most important determinants of health and longevity will be the personal choices made by each individual' (Cooper 1989:322). If the right choices are to be made in lifestyle there has to be a process of education. Cooper comments:

> 'So now is the time to instil those healthy habits in your children, while they're still young and their minds, appetites, and exercise patterns are still malleable. One of the greatest gifts parents can pass on

to their offspring is a more complete knowledge of
how their bodies operate – and an understanding of
what they can do to increase their chances of living out
their full life span in good spirits and good health'
(*ibid* 315).

Such education would ensure a healthy survival.

Dr Paul Kezdi observes:

'Man . . . in his early days . . . shared [the survival
instinct] with all other occupants of the planet. But
that was long ago. Today, of all the species of the
earth, man is the only one that repeatedly fails to make
proper use of his instincts. And this situation is
worsening in the Western world, despite all the
powerful and ever increasing efforts of medical science
in recent years to make man aware of the fact that
preventive maintenance of his body, and especially of
his heart, is the only way to assure a long and healthy
life. And all this despite the fact that the basic rules of
preventive health care are often no more than common
sense' (Kezdi 1981:15, 16).

It may be common sense, but we have been slow to adopt the
preventive measures which have been promoted for a good
one hundred years, especially in the area of diet and health.

Establishing a Nutrition Science

As Coon notes, 'Little was known of nutrition in those
days [the latter half of the nineteenth century]. Cornell
University's late professor of nutrition Dr Clive McCay dated
the genesis of modern nutritional science no earlier than
1900' (Coon 1993:11). Sylvester Graham and Russell Trall
had attempted to put nutrition on a scientific footing but it
was Kellogg who carried the work forward.

Reid stated that 'In the 1860s even scientists knew little of
modern human nutrition, and the public had only folklore
for guidance' (Reid 1982:138). It is significant then that the
obituary issue of *Good Health* following Kellogg's death

reported: 'The per capita consumption of flesh foods has been reduced fifty per cent during the last half century. Dr Kellogg has had more than a small part in bringing about the wholesome change in the dietary habits of the American people' (GH. 1944:9). Schwarz comments, 'If Kellogg did not succeed in converting all Americans to a vegetarian diet and in persuading them to discard coffee, tea, alcoholic beverages, and tobacco, it was not because he did not make a major effort in that direction' (Schwarz 1970:245). Kellogg's writings and experiments ensured that scientists and the general public had ample opportunity to learn nutrition.

Kellogg, in the book which was described by philosopher Will Durant as deserving of the Nobel Prize (Schwarz 1964:236), wrote of his own efforts in the promotion of dietary reform:

'There is perhaps no place in the world where the successive steps of scientific progress in the knowledge of nutrition and dietetics have been watched with greater care and interest than at Battle Creek Sanitarium. For more than forty years this institution has been a great clinical laboratory in which an intensive study of foodstuffs and of their effect upon the human body has been continuously carried on by the writer and his associates. . . . It is not claimed that complete knowledge has yet been attained. . . . the writer desires to ask the reader's consideration of the fact that however widely the ideas and methods herein presented may differ from those current in popular and professional usage, they cannot be justly looked upon as simply theoretical or experimental, since they are in daily and successful practical use in a large institution, in the development of which during the last forty-five years they are believed to have been the most important factor. However novel the methods presented may seem to some readers, they are by no means new; they are based upon biologic principles which are as old as the human race and only need a fair trial to demonstrate their value' (Kellogg 1921).

Horace B. Powell comments, 'Though the Doctor may have seemed revolutionary to his more conservative colleagues, he actually was restating and implementing basic health ideas which had been in the minds of men for several centuries' (Powell 1956:55).

In 1980 the *Dietary Guidelines for Americans* was published by the US Departments of Agriculture and Health, Education and Welfare. Robert E. Kowalski writes, 'That report suggests eating a wide variety of foods, avoiding too much fat, saturated fat, and cholesterol, eating foods with adequate starch and fibre, and avoiding too much sugar and sodium. That seems like good advice; everyone can live without feeling like a martyr. Then, as needed, fat intake can be further reduced' (Kowalski 1990:45). He also suggests giving up smoking and monitoring vitamin and mineral levels (*ibid*) 45, 46).

Kellogg's dietary advice would not have been out of place if it had been included in the report, as a brief look at his discussion of dietary components will indicate, of:

Protein – Kellogg recommended milk as the protein source and suggested that milk along with grains, fruits and vegetables would provide the body's protein needs. Eggs might be taken sparingly but not at all if milk was included in the diet. Eggs should be fresh, wholesome, free-range, and from well-fed hens.

Fats – Kellogg wrote that fats were the 'least essential food elements' (Kellogg 1921:842). He especially recommended olive oil used on salads, thus reducing the need for other fats in the diet. Butter he considered superior to margarine. Kellogg was against what he called 'bogus' butter – oleomargarine (Kellogg 1880:298, 299). [He might have changed his mind if he were still alive, given the wide range and types of margarine available today]. Fats used in the production of margarine in his day would not have been considered healthy generally. Interestingly, barely a decade ago, a report declared that 'Women who eat margarine are more prone to heart attacks' (Dover

1993). It is thought that the hardening process may have reduced the anticipated health benefits.

Carbohydrates – These should be largely from whole grains and potatoes. The value of these complex carbohydrates has been recognised in recent years. Current thinking is also in line with Kellogg's recommendation that the refined foods be avoided, with white bread being discarded in favour of either Graham bread or bran bread. Graham bread is a high-fibre bran bread formulated now as crackers.

Minerals & Vitamins – Kellogg recommended that adequate supplies be obtained from natural sources preferably using uncooked foods as a part of every meal.

Fibre – 'Roughage must be provided for every meal. Fresh fruit, greens, fresh vegetables, and especially bran or agar, in liberal quantities, should be used, not daily only, but at every meal' (*ibid*). Agar is an indigestible extract of seaweed used as a thickener and stabiliser, so contributing to fibre roughage.

Under the heading 'Balancing the Bill of Fare' Kellogg summarised his dietary recommendations (*ibid* 844). Each meal should contain a proper proportion of the food groups. He said that the protein needed to be adequate but warned against excess intake, listing among the consequences arteriosclerosis, *angina pectoris* and apoplexy. He stated, 'An excess of protein imposes another great burden upon the body by flooding the blood and tissue fluids with highly virulent toxins which raise blood pressure' (*ibid*). Kellogg also warned against an excess of fat and a superfluity of food salts and vitamins. He further warned of a constant danger of fibre deficiency.

Caroline Walker and Geoffrey Cannon note that Kellogg was not only a wholefood prescriber but also a manufacturer (Walker 1985:85, 86). It is this last point that has made Kellogg a household name worldwide.

Health Food Manufacturer

Two considerations led Kellogg to experiment with cereal
foods. Firstly, while a medical student in 1874-5, and
presumably pressed for time himself, he became convinced
that ready-to-eat cereals would fill a widespread need; and,
secondly, he wanted to provide a healthy dietary regime for
the patients at the Sanitarium.

Kellogg attributed the origin of the cereal food industry in
the United States to an immigrant worker from Hamburg,
Germany, named Ferdinand Shoemaker who had, as an
apprentice to a pharmacist in his homeland, been set the task
of grinding oatmeal for use in gruels and porridges. Settling
later in Akron, Ohio, he started a commercial venture,
resulting in the widespread acceptance of grain for dietary
use other than by the sick (Kellogg 1912:1579).

All good inventions are said to be chance discoveries, and
wheat and cornflakes are no exception. There is some doubt
on the part of biographers as to who actually discovered the
method by which cereal flakes are made. Some writers opt
for J. H. Kellogg (Kellogg 1921:257), others for his brother
Will (Johns 1977:87), and yet others for Kellogg's wife Ella
(Hessel 1992:15). In fact it was probably a joint effort and
certainly extended over a period of time, moving from the
limited facilities of Ella Kellogg's household kitchen to the
more commodious surroundings of the experimental
sanitarium kitchen before the technique was perfected, and
thence to a small factory set up for the purpose. Kellogg's
inventive genius did not stop at breakfast cereals but included
other cereal-and-nut-based-preparations to be used as
substitutes for animal proteins.

Kellogg describes these new products: 'The new diet is
good; *it looks good, it is savoury, it tastes good* in the mouth,
and it behaves well in the stomach. It makes good blood,
strong muscles, good brains, and is conducive to *good nature*,
good spirits, and the highest type of wholesome and righteous
living' (Kellogg 1912:1584). 'The new diet will work a

reformation not only in the kitchen, but in your stomach, in your heart, in your whole life, and in your home' (*ibid* 1585). The motivation behind all these products was to find a 'food which will make ill folks well, and will prevent well folks from becoming ill' (Stoltz 1992:4). Kellogg 'looked at the cereal business primarily as a means to support his missionary work, including endeavours as diverse as Battle Creek College and the Race Betterment Foundation' (*ibid* 5).

In no time at all others were making health food, with as many as one hundred and fifty businesses in Battle Creek alone. The proliferation of businesses and the similarity of products caused Stoltz to ask, 'Did [C. W.] Post steal *Grape Nuts* from *Granola*? Did Kellogg, in turn, steal *Granola* from *Granola* creator Dr James Caleb Jackson? Did Post steal *Postum* from Kellogg's *Caromel Cereal Coffee*?' Historian Ross Coller says, 'No', asserting that cereal product development 'was an evolution and improvement. As it turned out, each product was better than its predecessor' (*ibid*:7).

Kellogg's brother William Keith Kellogg took over the cereal business and made it the world's largest cereal company and the breakfast-food industry a multi-million-dollar enterprise. Kellogg retained the other businesses associated with the Sanitarium. Although he expected loyalty from those working in his companies – even to the signing of a promise not to divulge technical knowledge to competitors – (*ibid*) he often gave recipes to his audiences. He stated, 'You may say that I am destroying the health food business here by giving those recipes, but I am not after the business, I am after the reform; that is what I want to see' (*ibid*:8). The money that he made through the business was spent on promoting his programme of biologic living. As he said, 'What is money for except to make the whole world better, to help people have a better life?' (Schwarz 1964:85).

His dietary regime as taught and as produced through his health-food factories would be to no avail if there were no associated lifestyle change in the individuals concerned.

Unless people changed, disease would be inevitable. The two most prominent lifestyle diseases that his diet and health reform programme helped were heart disease and cancer.

Heart Disease

It would be gratifying to report that Kellogg had a well-defined programme designed to combat heart disease. If that had been so, he would have been a visionary! As Schwarz notes, 'Relatively few Americans in the first part of the nineteenth century lived long enough to be plagued with the degenerative organic diseases which trouble their descendants today' (Coon 1993:11). Heart disease is a relatively recent condition. Werbach writes, 'Few people realise that coronary arteriosclerosis, the major cause of cardiovascular death, is a disease of the twentieth century. It was unrecognised before 1890 and was virtually unknown until sixty or seventy years ago' (Werbach 1986:22).

The risk factors for heart disease include: age, person's sex, heredity, high blood fats (triglyceride, cholesterol levels), hypertension, obesity, inactivity, smoking, stress, and diabetes. In dealing with these Kellogg would have taken the same view as that outlined by Dr Russell Gibbs: 'If we are to look at coronary heart disease from a preventive aspect it can only be by eradicating those factors that predispose to its development' (Gibbs 1979:18).

Heart disease is the most frequent cause of death and disability in the Western world including the United Kingdom. In fact death from heart and vascular disease accounts for nearly half of all fatalities from whatever sources. It causes at least as many deaths as all other major killers added together.

While not formulating a specific coronary heart-disease programme, Kellogg at one time or another addressed all of the coronary risk factors. Whorton notes that by the 1900s vegetarians were already linking a meat diet to cardiovascular disease (Whorton 1982:236). Kellogg's earliest writings concern the purifying of the blood, employing the natural remedies which would prove effective for a wide range of conditions. The regimen promoted would in fact have been very appropriate for either prevention or rehabilitation:

> 'The most important means of purifying the blood – whatever vendors of "purifiers" may say – are the free use of pure air, a clean skin, a sound liver, active kidneys, exercise, and getting the system into its natural state. One may purify the blood more in a single day while breathing pure air than by taking sarsaparilla [a medicinal root] for a month. More of effete matter is thrown off by exercise and perspiration in one day – more than one half of all taken into the stomach, solid and liquid – than by a year's dosing with some of the nostrums of the groceries [grocers' shops where patent medicines could be bought]. A free use of fruits will stimulate the liver to filter out more waste or 'bile' than some suppose; while good, plain and wholesome food will make good blood, the old and worn-out materials pass off by the means referred to, soon leaving the body in a good state. Pure air and water for cleansing are cheaper than the "patent blood purifiers", and will effect far more' (Kellogg 1879:26).

The language of the statement quoted is a bit quaint but the sentiments are sound and underwent development quite quickly. As we see in an article headed *Tobacco a Cause of Heart Disease*, written in 1880, Kellogg adopts a much more clinical approach to the condition.

> 'The effect of tobacco upon the heart is indicated by the pulse, which is a most accurate index to the condition of the heart. The pulse of the tobacco-user says, in terms as plain as any words could, that his heart is partially paralysed, that its force and vigour are diminished, that it is, in fact, poisoned. Old smokers, and not a few of those who have indulged but a few years, often suffer with palpitations of the heart, intermittent pulse, angina pectoris, and other

Dr John Harvey Kellogg, whose scientific approach to the wonders of life brought a new orthodoxy to health reform, formerly the domain of many outlandish ideas.

Will Keith Kellogg, the long-suffering brother whose business acumen kept the doctor organised and financially successful, and who, when he left his brother's employ, founded the most successful breakfast food empire ever.

Through their various
business ventures and
legal tussles Kellogg and
Charles W. Post, of
'Postum' fame, brought
the health food industry
to prominence.

Dr Kellogg's wife,
Ella E. Easton.

Christmas

1852 —   1853 — 1920

Nineteen Hundred and Twenty-seven

Kellogg wrote fifty-seven books. Many,
including his *Domestic Hygiene* were
over 1,500 pages. He also wrote
thousands of articles for papers and
magazines.

Kellogg kept abreast of and used innovations in
technology. He held the first known transatlantic
telephone conversation advising a doctor in
Monte Carlo.

Ever the popular
speaker, Kellogg in his
famous white suit
enjoyed lecturing to the
health guests and in
particular answering
questions from the
Monday Night Question
Box.

The Health Reform Institute just grew and grew.
In 1876 it comprised 100 beds and had eight
buildings on fifteen acres.

Fire, need, and prosperity meant that the Western Reform Institute was continully changing its appearance and name and in the process becoming the largest medical institution in the northern hemisphere as the Battle Creek Sanitarium.

Started in 1927, the Towers Addition expanded sanitarium facilities to accommodate 1,300 guests. Then came 1929 and the Depression. The average number of patients fell to 300 in 1930, and in 1933 the institution went into receivership. Battle Creek Sanitarium moved to smaller quarters.

Will Keith's advertising ideas, always well ahead of the
pack, ensured that Kellogg was a household name.

The beginings of Kellogg's extended family of fostered and adopted children which eventually numbered forty-two.

Dr Russell T. Trall
(1812 – 1877)

Drs Gertrude and Edwin Brown, fellow pioneers of
Dr Kellogg, who travelled hundreds of miles on the
rocky roads of Ireland, where they spent nine happy
years in the early 1900s. Together they later
established the Crieff Nursing Home in Scotland.

Dr Gertrude Brown in
1970. Dr Brown was
matron of the Battle Creek
Sanitarium during the
height of its popularity and
fame in the 1920s.

Crieff Nursing Home, now part of the Roundelwood Health Spa Complex. Situated in one of the most beautiful locations in Scotland, Roundelwood offers a programme of health improvement with emphasis on the whole person, total lifestyle. Email: *health@roundelwood.freeserve.co.uk*

The original Battle Creek Sanitarium building (destroyed by fire in 1902) was finally succeeded by this less extravagent building in 1924.

symptoms of derangement of this most important
organ. There is, in fact, a diseased condition of the
heart which is so characteristic of chronic tobacco
poisoning that it has been very appropriately termed
"narcotism of the heart". Medical statistics show that
about one in every four smokers has this condition.
There is good evidence for believing that not only
functional but organic disease of the heart may be
occasioned by the use of tobacco' (Kellogg 1880:40).

Kellogg later elaborated on tobacco and heart disease in
his book *Tobaccoism* (1937), where he reported from his
own case studies that forty-three per cent of smokers had
arteriosclerosis of the coronary arteries even in the 20- to 30-
year age range (Kellogg 1937:61). Evidently by 1937 Kellogg
had made a close study of heart disease and had by 1913
introduced the newly-invented electro-cardiograph to Battle
Creek.

One of Kellogg's major volumes, *The New Dietetics*
(1921), had a chapter devoted to *Diet in Disease of the Heart
and Blood Vessels – cardio-vascular – Renal Disease*, thus
indicating the growing focus of attention on the subject. His
dietary information had, by this time, become very specific.
Kellogg even mentions the effect of caffeine on the heart, '2
to 10 grains will produce the most violent excitement of the
vascular and nervous systems – palpitation of the heart,
extraordinary frequency, irregularity, and often intermission
of the pulse . . .' (Kellogg 1921:450), and 'Tea, coffee, and
the whole family of caffein[e]-containing drugs must be
regarded as poisons which especially affect the heart and
blood-vessels' (*ibid* 453). He quotes a number of
contemporary scientific authorities confirming the link
between various heart disorders and caffeine.

Modern medicine has slowly recognised the link between
diet and heart disease. Dr Eugene B. Mozes, commenting on
more recent treatment methods, wrote, 'The year 1955 will
probably turn out to have been the turning point in the
treatment of heart attack. Until that time, physicians had

prescribed six-week bed rest, lying flat on the back absolutely motionless, for every patient. In that year two studies were published which proved that such [a] regimen was not only not necessary but may have been actually harmful in some cases' (Mozes 1959:11). By May 1959, the link was growing stronger. Dr Levin Waters, of the Department of Pathology, Yale University School of Medicine, said, 'There is now voluminous epidemiological, clinical, and experimental evidence that diet and the level of lipids in the blood are associated in some way with the development of arteriosclerosis. . . . Most of this evidence is associated in nature . . . . Although so urgently needed, little direct information of the genesis of arteriosclerosis in relation to diet and to lipids exists' (Marvin 1960:148). That situation changed quite quickly. In a short while Dr Katz and colleagues were able to report that 'virtually no evidence has been presented contradicting the thesis that patterns of cholesterolaemia (excessive amounts of cholesterol in the blood) in the United States population are a resultant of life-span habitual diets. Nor have any other hypotheses been advanced to account for these patterns of cholesterolaemia' (*ibid* 154).

Diet modification and the introduction of a vegetarian diet of the kind promoted by Kellogg have been demonstrated to be effective in controlling heart disease. Rene Noorbergen noted that a 3 June 1961 editorial of the *Journal of the American Medical Association* commenting on research work done by Dr W. A. Thomas *et al* stated: ' "A vegetarian diet can prevent 90 per cent of our thrombo-embolic disease and 97 per cent of our coronary occlusions". *This means that a proper vegetarian diet can help prevent 90 per cent* of all clots in veins and arteries, and that no less than 97 *per cent of all heart attacks* can be prevented by living on a *meatless diet!'* (Noorbergen 1975:41). Dr Peter Sleight observes, 'In the United Kingdom we have often overtly or covertly poked fun at the American obsession with health during the last decade. However, the recent trends in mortality from vascular disease in the United States suggest that this campaign is at last beginning to bite and there appears to be a reduction' (Kezdi 1981:8).

A position paper on vegetarian diets published by the American Dietetic Association now states:

> 'Studies indicate that vegetarians often have lower morbidity and mortality rates . . . . Not only is mortality from coronary artery disease lower in vegetarians than in nonvegetarians, but vegetarian diets have also been successful in arresting coronary artery disease. Scientific data suggest positive relationships between a vegetarian diet and reduced risk for . . . obesity, coronary artery disease, hypertension, diabetes mellitus, and some types of cancer' (Robbins:15).

These studies include the work done by Dr Dean Ornish and his colleagues which showed that diet and lifestyle not only arrested coronary artery disease but could reverse it (Ornish 1990:129-133). Dr William Castelli, the Director of the now-famed Framingham Health Study, says, 'Vegetarians have the best diet; they have the lowest rates of coronary heart disease of any group in the country' (Robbins:19).

Data from the McDougall Programme located at St Helena Hospital (in the Napa Valley, California, and itself one of the direct successors to the Battle Creek vision) involving over 1,000 participants show

> 'Blood pressure fell within hours of starting the (very low-fat vegan diet) McDougall Programme. Twenty per cent of the people were on blood pressure medications the day they began the programme. In almost every case the medications were stopped that day. Yet the blood pressure dropped (significantly) by the second day' (*ibid*:30).

Kellogg would have been delighted by these observations and the science which supported them. What has been accomplished for heart disease by lifestyle modification has also been successful in reducing cancer rates.

Cancer

It is said that the cancer situation in the United States is getting worse rather than better and that Americans now have almost a one in three chance of contracting the condition (Werbach 1986:23). The link between diet and cancer is even stronger than that of diet and heart disease.

Thomas A. Davis, commenting on the conjoint report produced by the National Research Council and the National Academy of Sciences of the United States, says, 'Present evidence suggests that most common cancers are influenced by diet; some researchers estimated that diet contributes to from 30 to 60 per cent of all cancer' (Davis 1982:4). The report implicates fats – both saturated and unsaturated, and certain types of meat – salt-cured, salt-pickled, and smoked. Strongly recommended were the cruciferous vegetables – cabbages, turnips, cauliflowers, sprouts, and radishes – as they contain vitamins A or C. These appeared to reduce susceptibility to cancers, particularly cancers affecting the urinary bladder, large bowel, skin, lungs, stomach and oesophagus. The report counselled against taking vitamin supplements, preferring that these protective agents be taken in the natural state (*ibid*). The National Academy of Sciences in a document supporting the report in the same year stated that Americans 'may prevent almost 50 per cent of all cancers by controlling what they eat. The Chairman of the joint panel, Dr Clifford Grobstein, said, 'The evidence is increasingly impressive that what we eat does affect our chances of getting cancer' (AH. 1982:6). These and similar reports led to the European Communities Commission issuing their own report and programme 'Europe Against Cancer' launched in 1990. The EAC report confirms that around sixty per cent of cancers are controllable and makes similar recommendations to those contained in the American reports, where it is claimed that their 10 point code for living can reduce the risk of cancer:

Certain Cancers May Be Avoided

Do not smoke. Smokers, stop as quickly as possible and do not smoke in the presence of others.

Moderate your consumption of alcoholic drinks, beers, wines and spirits.

Avoid excessive exposure to the sun.

Follow health and safety instructions at work, concerning production, handling and use of any substance which may cause cancer.

Your general health will benefit from the following two commandments which may also reduce the risks of some cancers:

Frequently eat fresh fruits and vegetables, and cereals with a high fibre content.

Avoid becoming overweight and limit your intake of fatty foods.

More Cancers Will Be Cured If Detected Early

See a doctor if you notice a lump, or observe a change in a mole, or abnormal bleeding.

See a doctor if you have persistent problems, such as a persistent cough, a persistent hoarseness, a change in bowel habits or an unexplained weight loss.

For Women

Have a cervical smear regularly.

Check your breasts frequently and, if possible, undergo mammography at systematic intervals above the age of 50 (Kreuter *et al* 1990:3).

It seems strange to see a little health reform language creeping into the recommendations with two referred to as 'commandments' of health. These two involve dietary change (Walsh 1990:8).

Kellogg would have been delighted with all these reports vindicating the position that he had taken for so many years. Despite the fact that there is still much dietary disagreement, the status of certain foods in the disease process is now quite well documented. Dr Peter Slight highlights this, saying, 'Although there is a good deal of controversy about diet, there is no doubt that our national eating habits have changed profoundly in the last 25 years, and we do take much more of our diet as fat compared with carbohydrate than formerly' (Kezdi 1981:8). A flesh diet contributes a major portion of dietary fat. Many researchers believe that changing to a vegetarian or semi-vegetarian diet would help to lower cancer rates, a view to which Kellogg subscribed.

Cyril Scott writing in 1957, and quoting Kellogg, stated:

'An anti-toxic diet, that is, a diet which discourages the development of putrefactive poisons in the intestine, is especially to be commended as a means of combating cancer . . . .

'Dr Kellogg went on to say that during the last 45 years he had unusual opportunities for observing "the influence of a non-flesh dietary upon the occurrence of cancer." And considering that well over 100,000 patients have been treated by Dr Kellogg's sanatorium [sic], his conclusions cannot be dismissed as negligible. Especially as he further states that of the many thousand of flesh abstainers with whom he had been acquainted, he had only come across four cases of cancer in persons who had been vegetarians over a long period. Dr Kellogg pointed out that a "liberal use should be made of fresh fruit and vegetables, *because of the large amount of potash* they contain" ' (Scott 1957:41).

Kellogg evidently wrote a letter to a Mr Ellis Barker in 1924 in which he said, 'The head nurse of the Cancer Hospital of New York told me that it is a common thing to see great improvement in patients coming there, even in cases of secondary cancer, after being put on a *strict non-flesh regime*' (*ibid* 42; MacKenzie n.d.45).

Framingham's Dr Castelli comments, 'Now some people scoff at vegetarians, but they have only 40 per cent of our cancer rate. They outlive us. On average they outlive other men by about six years now' (Robbins 2001:39). A *British Medical Journal* statement confirms Castelli's view: 'What is remarkable about the diet-cancer story is the consistency with which certain foods emerge as important in reducing risks across the range of cancers. Millions of cancer cases could be prevented each year if more individuals adopted diets low in meat and high in fruits and vegetables' (*ibid*:40).

Kellogg's interest was not only in diet but lifestyle and the combined effect of these on the disease process. As Dr Jan W. Kuzma states, 'Differences in mortality between vegetarians and nonvegetarians should not be considered primarily a result of not eating meat, but more likely of differences in a range of lifestyle habits' (Kuzma 1989:16).

Adventist Lifestyle

We can know that Kellogg had an influence on the national Research Council, the National Academy of Sciences, and the ECC reports indirectly at least. Kuzma observes that over the past twenty-nine years more than one hundred and fifty-seven articles in various scientific journals have reported on the Adventist lifestyle which Kellogg did so much to shape (*ibid*).

Doctors Frank Lemon, Richard Walden, and P. William Dysinger started the scientific interest in 1958 when they reported that the incidence of heart disease and cancer was significantly lower in Californian Seventh-day Adventists than in Californians of comparable age (*ibid*). This led to other studies using Seventh-day Adventists either in direct experimentation or as a control group for studies taking place elsewhere. The Loma Linda, California, studies conducted by Lemon *et al* showed that cancer deaths were thirty per cent less than might be expected, and coronary heart disease deaths were one third lower in Seventh-day Adventist vegetarians.

The Adventist lifestyle has been acclaimed worldwide. One American scientist commented, 'It appears that the best insurance one can take out today is to follow the lifestyle of SDAs' (*ibid* 17). A Canadian official said, 'I've got some advice on how to improve the health of Canadians, and, at the same time, lop billions of dollars off our annual costs. I think we should study the lifestyle of adherents of the Seventh-day Adventist Church and then explore ways and means of persuading the public to emulate the Adventists in at least some ways' (*ibid*). When the United States Congress examined guidelines for the health of the nation they utilised findings on Adventists, referring to the lifestyle as the 'Adventist advantage' (*ibid*).

World authority on hypertension Dr Norman M. Kaplan, of the University of Texas Southwestern Medical School at Dallas, told Adventist health professionals, 'You as Adventists may have espoused a certain dietary lifestyle on the basis of faith [through the influence of Ellen G. White], in the past; but now you can practise it on the basis of scientific evidence [through the influence of Kellogg and the professionals who have followed him]. Hopefully you will not go back and rejoin the mainstream again, but rather adhere to your health heritage' (Coon 1993:12). Dr William Herbert Foege, an assistant US Surgeon General, declared, 'You Adventists are now the role model for the rest of the world' (*ibid*). It might be argued that Kellogg's greatest impact on health promotion is to be found in the lifestyle of approximately twelve million Seventh-day Adventists worldwide and their further influence through the church's community health promotion programmes. Schwarz comments, 'Although he spent the last third of his life outside the Adventist Church, Kellogg's personal contributions to that denomination's growth were great' (Schwarz 1970:244).

Kellogg's early writings and consistent medical practice at Battle Creek showed his interest in internal medicine. Many of his *Good Health* articles featured the digestive system. Elmer McCullum in his *A History of Nutrition* [Boston 1957, pages 123-127] cites several of Kellogg's studies from Battle Creek. Schwarz writes that Kellogg's 'repeated calls for moderation in eating, . . . undoubtedly played a part in initiating the continuing investigation into the relationship between proper weight and good health' (*ibid*). Unusual for the age, Kellogg's dietary works invariably included tables showing the calorific values of foods, weight tables, and ideal foods for special diets.

Solitary vice

If there is one area of lifestyle where Kellogg has attracted the most criticism, it is in the area of sex education and in particular the perils of masturbation or 'solitary vice' as it was known.

John Money, Director of Johns Hopkins Medical School psychohormonal research unit, can say nothing good about Kellogg in respect of sex education (and even accuses the whole cornflake philosophy as a thumbs down for sex!) He claims that all of Kellogg's writings on the subject are sex-negative and labels this area of Kellogg's life 'Kellogg's folly':

> 'Kellogg's folly has its counterpart in those masterpieces of Victorian architectural conceit that had bankrupted their builders. Never completed they have names like Burton's Folly. The master plan had failed. Either some of the essential parts had been omitted, or the parts had failed to synthesize into a whole in proper sequence. Kellogg's folly was a challenge – a failed medical theory that needed to be analyzed' (Money 1985:14).

Money claims that Kellogg's folly was due in part to his being unqualified to write on the subject of sex and calls Kellogg's own sexuality into question. He speculates that Sylvester Graham's restrictive theories of sex justified Kellogg's own aversion; that Kellogg's marriage to Ella E. Eaton was not consummated, and that he spent his honeymoon writing an antisex book; that the Kelloggs had separate bedrooms; and that the regular daily enema that Kellogg had could be symptomatic of klismaphilia 'an anomaly of sexual and erotic functioning traceable to childhood, in which an enema substitutes for regular intercourse' (*ibid*: 83, 84).

Whatever Kellogg's personal sexual status, he would probably have argued that he was defending what episcopal bishop of Edinburgh, Richard Holloway, would later call the 'developed Christian tradition' in which 'sex was itself harmful and morally problematic; it was the means whereby sin entered human nature, so it had to be hedged about with protective mechanisms' (Holloway 1999:58).

Kellogg's seemingly puritanical approach – his protective mechanisms – was in keeping with the age and acted as a counterbalance to the licentious behaviour of the prevailing *Free Sex Movement* seen in such groups as the Oneida Community that flourished during the mid-nineteenth century when Kellogg was a young man.

John Humphrey Noyes (1811-1886) had introduced what he called 'complex marriage' in the New England community, where instead of polygamy he had advocated a system, omnigamy, where any man or woman could come together at will. Noyes was also interested in eugenics, but unlike Kellogg's race betterment through good health, he promoted 'stirpiculture', controlled reproduction, and as the means to achieve his aims taught *karezza* or *coitus obstructus,* his unacknowledged adaptation of Tantric sex (Tannahill 1992:413, 414).

Kellogg's thirty-nine signs of solitary vice leading to gross mental and physical disorders are the special objects of

Money's vented anger. He finds it absurd that sexual abstinence is still encouraged premaritally in Adventist colleges and medical education, but the degree to which one accepts Money's views will depend on where one draws one's personal line in the proverbial sand. His statement that 'In 1898 an antimasturbation food and extinguisher of sexual desire was invented – namely, Kellogg's Corn Flakes!' may say more about Money than about Kellogg!

History has shown that the dire warnings concerning the effects of masturbation were largely unfounded; so one can agree with Money in one respect when he says,

> 'What is more remarkable [than Kellogg's outrageous views] is that he lived until 1943 and did not, with age, have the professional courage to admit that formerly he had been wrong' (*ibid*:97).

It is easy to make the remark with hindsight. How many people do admit that they are wrong? In any case the pace of Kellogg's life, even to its end, gave him plenty of other things to think about.

Physical Therapies

Diet and lifestyle absorbed Kellogg's interest as he promoted the value of biologic living. 'Dr Kellogg's scientific medical training led him to investigate and to demonstrate the physiological effect of . . . heat, electricity, hydrotherapy, and corrective exercise. To a large extent,' as Schwarz points out, 'it was Kellogg and his colleagues at the Battle Creek Sanitarium who gave professional respectability to the wide variety of therapeutic measure employed by today's specialists in physical therapy' (*ibid*).

These were certainly areas in which Kellogg excelled. Doctors Agatha and Calvin Thrash state of Kellogg and the Battle Creek Sanitarium:

> 'The reason people kept the 1,200-bed institution filled was that the treatments encompassed the best of the several different schools of the healing arts and

avoided their harmful aspects . . . . The physicians
were master physiologists, far in advance of physicians
of later years. The Battle Creek Sanitarium developed
hydrotherapy to its greatest degree in modern times.
Dr John Harvey Kellogg was known world-wide for
his use of hydrotherapy' (Thrash 1981:5).

The Thrashes also indicate that hydrotherapy was a respected
treatment in the United States (*ibid* 6), a status that it did not
always have elsewhere.

Kellogg's book *Rational Hydrotherapy: A Manual of the
Physiologic and Therapeutic Effects of Hydriatic Procedures,
and the Technique of Their Application in the Treatment of
Disease* (1901), was for many years the standard textbook on
the subject in physiotherapy schools. He also wrote other
books related to various aspects of physical therapy.

Thomas Edison perfected the electric light bulb in 1891.
By 1895 Kellogg was using electricity for a variety of
therapeutic purposes. Observing that the heat from a light
bulb helped relieve the asthmatic symptoms of a colleague,
Dr Kate Lindsay, led Kellogg to develop radiant heat
equipment and heat cabinets still employed in physiotherapy
departments (Abbott 1941:22,23), and recently exciting
interest in scientific journals (New Scientist 2001:105).

Kellogg was also a pioneer in exercise therapy. It was he
rather than Dr Kenneth H. Cooper who invented aerobics,
contrary to Cooper's claim, 'I introduced aerobics as a new
concept of exercise' (Cooper 1970:5)! Cooper describes the
exercise regimen: 'Aerobics is a system of exercise designed to
improve your overall health, but particularly the condition of
the heart, lungs and blood vessels' (*ibid* 169). Schwarz
comments, 'Nearly a century before the *Reader's Digest* gave
wide publicity to the US Air Force's new exercise programme
called Aerobics, Dr Kellogg made the same claims about the
therapeutic value of exercise' (Schwarz 1970:51). Kellogg's
exercise programme called for activity vigorous enough to
induce free perspiration and maintained long enough to
produce fatigue. This could be accomplished by Swedish

exercise of the callisthenic type, walking, cycling – which Kellogg practised – or swimming. The earlier the exercise was started in life, the better would be the results. Kellogg recommended that 'Children's games, bicycle riding, and swimming are especially commended as excellent exercises for children, . . . Every child should learn to swim. Special attention should be given to the development of lung power and to the cultivation of a good physique and correct carriage of the body in walking and sitting' (Kellogg 1912:1615).

Kellogg developed exercise machines, including the universal dynamometer which helped to measure strength and endurance. He compiled tables of norms and permitted deviations for different physiques which were used not only to establish the fitness levels of the Sanitarium patients but also for military medicals. His equipment and tables were used at the Westpoint Military Academy and the naval Academy at Annapolis (GH.1944:11). For the general public Kellogg made exercise records marketed by the Columbia Gramophone Company in the early 1920s (Schwarz 1970:51).

Believing the Message

If Kellogg seemed to be obsessed with health reform in all of its multi-facets, it was because he believed in the reality of his utopian thinking and had the faith to practise it. Dr Gertrude Brown, who was herself the oldest practising physician in the United Kingdom at the age of ninety-three (working in Crieff, Scotland), and who had earlier served as the matron of the Battle Creek Sanitarium under the leadership of Kellogg, wrote, 'Throughout those long years Dr Kellogg maintained that vision of health education, and was a pioneer in various lines of medical work. Leading men of the world acclaimed him. Sir [William] Arbuthnot Lane [1856-1943] told me in London that Dr Kellogg was the greatest medical man of his generation. He said it would take fifty years at least for the medical profession to realise and appreciate the great contribution he had made to medical knowledge, and that wise medical men – including Lane – were following hard on his heels' (Brown n.d.:91). The close association of Kellogg and Lane is not without significance, as one writer describes the latter, 'Sir Arbuthnot Lane and other men who were not walking the stationary treadmill of orthodox research' (Scott 1957:37).

Frank Knox, Secretary of the US Navy at the time of Kellogg's death, wrote, 'The sudden passing of Dr Kellogg robs the country of one of its greatest individualists and leaders in medicine. His contribution to national health and well-being was very great and will be long remembered' (GH.1944:14). It is time now to see how Dr Kellogg made his contribution through the various avenues and media of his day.

The Media:
by Voice, Pen and Action

Kellogg's principal biographer, Richard W. Schwarz, states that 'Almost all aspects of Kellogg's biologic living appear in one form or another in the teachings of earlier health reformers and in the writings of Ellen White' (Schwarz 1970:54), and, 'Although Kellogg did not offer an original health regimen, the atmosphere in which he presented it was' (*ibid* 65).

To a great extent Kellogg himself helped to create that atmosphere. Around 1879 Dr Edward Cox, retiring president of the Calhoun County Medical Association, said of the Western Health Reform Institute at Battle Creek,

> 'During this decade the *Water Cure* was established at Battle Creek. It was not conducted on rational principles nor by competent men, was no credit to its founders nor to those who had it in charge, for they were partisan and irrational in all their doings. Our profession continued to improve through this decade up to 1870, since which time its history is as well known to all of you as to myself. I will, however, say that the Old Water Cure has been transformed into the "Sanitarium". It is now ably managed, and is a credit to its able chief and his accomplished assistants' (Cox 1879).

A high accolade indeed for a young man of 27. How had such changes come about in a few short years? Kellogg said, 'I consented to take charge on the condition that I should be permitted to completely reorganise the work and put it on a thoroughly scientific basis' (Kellogg 1938). He did this against his self-admitted handicap of youth and unimpressive personality.

The Sanitarium Concept

First of all, Kellogg weaned the institute away from the typical water cure of the time. He wrote, 'This institution is not a "water cure," neither does it employ, exclusively, any special method of treatment; but the plan upon which it is carried on is to employ *all remedial agents*, applying each to the cases of which it is especially adapted. All diseases are treated here in a thoroughly scientific manner, and with a degree of success unattainable under any other plan of treatment' (Kellogg 1876).

Later, writing about the establishment of the sanitarium, he described it as 'a scientific medical enterprise devoted forever to the public welfare' and that this was to be accomplished by pursuing five aims (Kellogg 1913:5):

'FIRST – To put into active, effective, and systematic use every practical method which modern science has provided for the accurate determination of deviations from the normal standard of health in structure or function, and for the estimation of the amount of such variation, so far as possible expressing these variations by means of coefficients, so as to make exact comparisons possible.

SECOND – To make available in most approved form every rational curative means known to medical science, so that the same may be brought to bear in any individual case, giving special prominence to physical therapy, or so-called physiologic therapeutics.

THIRD – To combine with the special professional, technical, and institutional advantages of the modern hospital the luxuries and comforts of the modern hotel, together with the genial atmosphere, security and freedom of the home.

FOURTH – To organise and carry forward various lines of research having for their purpose the improvement of the conditions of human life, especially in relation to diet and nutrition.

FIFTH – The organisation and maintenance of various charities, especially hospitals and dispensaries, for the treatment of the sick poor' (Kellogg 1913:5).

Moreover, this extensive and costly enterprise was itself set
up as a charity. Kellogg could have been a multi-millionaire
but was far more interested in reform than in money. As
writer Garth Stoltz comments, Kellogg's 'views regarding
profit were missionary, not mercenary' (Stoltz 1992:8). A
Citizen's committee investigating the charitable and
philanthropic objects of Kellogg's organisation stated that:

> 'The revelations made by our investigation have been a
> surprise to us. Not only were we personally unaware
> of the wholly philanthropic nature of the institution,
> under the law, but we were also unaware of the vast
> amount of charitable work performed by it, and the
> wonderful sacrifices made by the managers and
> employees generally. The large corp of physicians
> receive no professional fees, and only weekly wages so
> small that their services are practically a charity. This
> is also true of the hundreds of nurses and helpers.
> They are a band of sincere people, conscientiously
> devoting themselves to a great work for humanity, and
> not for personal gain. . . . The more deeply we have
> gone into the investigation, the more convincing and
> overwhelming the proofs have become of the
> straightforward management, the lofty purpose, the
> widespread devotion and wonderful self-sacrifice of
> the nearly one thousand personal [sic] employed in it'
> (Kellogg 1913:26, 27).

Kellogg proudly echoed the lavish praise of the 'charity
commissioners' in an article written in 1878: 'This institution
. . . has grown to be the largest institution of its kind in the
world. And if one seeks for more complete appliances and
facilities for treating all manner of diseases, and a more
intelligent application of them to cases in hand, he must seek
them on some other planet; for here we have the best that
this one affords'! (Kellogg 1878).

The Sanitarium Purpose

Michael Wilson, writing in 1975, said, 'Hospitals, in fact, are a school of life. . . . One of the lessons learnt in hospital is the nature of "health". . . . The primary task of the hospital can be described as: To enable patients, their families and staff to learn from the experience of illness and death how to build a healthy society' (Wilson 1975:94). Kellogg aspired to even greater heights: he determined the sanitarium to be a 'University of Health' – a place where people could learn to stay well (Whorton 1982:204, 205). As Kellogg wrote,

> 'Part of the work of a physician is the instruction of the people in matters pertaining to health and life. According to his idea, in the good time coming the treatment of the sick will largely consist of a scientific training of the whole body out of the ways of physical wrong-doing into the paths of physical uprightness. An invalid will be put through such a process of grooming, and dieting, and exercise, that he will verily be "born again", his maladies not antidoted, but left behind in the process of growth and vital progress which has been carried on' (Kellogg 1893:iii).

To quote again from Wilson as to how the reform in health will come about: 'Education for health is not simply an extra discipline similar to other clinical subjects. It is what health and illness are all about within the movement of man towards greatness. The first health educators in society are mothers of families' (Wilson 1975:102). Put more simply, 'Mothers create health or illness in their children by the information, attitudes and life-styles to which they introduce their children' (*ibid* 34). Eighty-two years before Wilson's statement Kellogg had said the same thing; 'State and national health boards and committees certainly do excellent work for communities and nations; but the real influence which they exercise over the health of individuals is insignificant when compared with that which may be, and indeed is, exercised by the matrons of the various households which make up villages, cities, and nations' (Kellogg 1893:17). Again put simply, 'All reforms must begin at home to be effective' (*ibid* 18). Not only the home but the school, 'He [the physician] will follow the children to the schoolroom, and insist upon the training of the body as well as the mind' (*ibid* iv).

Enthusiastic Speaker

Kellogg was not just a health theorist. He used the sanitarium as a lecture base for patients and visitors. His sanitarium lectures often took the form of answering questions left in a box provided for the purpose. He lectured groups comprising seventy-five to two hundred people at each session. Jonathan Penner in a Purdue University dissertation estimates that Kellogg gave about five thousand public lectures over a forty-year period, each lasting approximately one and a half to two hours, and delivered at the rate of one hundred and eighty to two hundred words a minute. He was reckoned to be not so much a brilliant speaker but rather an enthusiast for his subject (Schwarz 1964:199). Kellogg also lectured at the universities of Michigan, Stanford, Tuskeegee and Utah; the Boston College of Physicians and Surgeons; and in public lectures in the cities of Austin (where in 1910 he shared the platform with ex-President T. Roosevelt), Baltimore, Chattanooga, Dallas and Louisville (*ibid* 206).

Prolific Writer

In keeping with his idea of educating children intelligently with regard to health reform, Kellogg produced text books for secondary schools and colleges covering anatomy, physiology and hygiene. Harper Brothers commissioned primary grade texts from Kellogg and he also wrote upper grade texts for high school students for the American Book Company. In conjunction with Professor Michael Vincent O'Shea, of the University of Wisconsin, Kellogg wrote a series of books for the Macmillan Company.

Many of his books arose out of his work at Battle Creek and expounded more fully on subjects that he dealt with on a daily basis. The books varied in length from booklets to major volumes of about two thousand pages. In all, Kellogg wrote approximately fifty books [see appendix] as well as articles and editorials for the various journals of which he was either editor or regular contributor. Many of these books became best sellers. His *Hygienic Cook Book* sold approximately thirty thousand copies. His *New Dietetics* sold even more. A statement from Kellogg to a reporter in 1903 confirmed that he had annually received – for over twenty-five years – around eight to nine thousand dollars in royalties from his books (*ibid* 232, 235). Whorton says of his books that 'His volumes were the most elaborate defences of vegetarianism, the most scathing denunciations of alcohol, the most merciless attacks on sexual misconduct' (Whorton 1982:203, 204). Yet even Whorton has to admit the success of the *Good Health* which he describes as 'a popular journal, . . . which commanded an audience of more than twenty thousand subscribers at times, and continued in existence [beyond Kellogg's death in 1943] until 1955' (*ibid*).

Kellogg's record for uninterrupted dictation to his secretary, who had four assistants, was a twenty-hour stretch. He would use the night hours to translate foreign medical books for his own edification or write a book of his own around the clock until it was finished (Powell 1956:57). In a fifty-year period Kellogg established more than thirty companies and publications (*ibid* 60).

Kellogg's Writing Style

The vast output of writing is an evidence of the passion that Kellogg channelled into his work, causing him to use the kind of language for which Whorton criticises him. Kellogg was nothing if not direct in his speech and, it has to be remembered, spoke with the moral tone of his age. He could, however, modify his speech or writing to suit his audience. To a group of church conference delegates he adopted a strong moral tone when he said,

> 'The great majority of maladies are the result of poisons in the human system. A person whose stomach is poisoned, is not a perfectly sane man; he is living under a cloud, he is in an incubus all the time. He cannot think clearly, cannot be as good a Christian as he ought to be, cannot discern moral principles as well as he ought. The brain is not able to work with great quickness, clearness, and accuracy. Certainly if a man cannot add up a column of figures without making a mistake, he does not have that moral clearness which he ought to have in distinguishing between right and wrong. It is absolutely impossible . . . . We cannot possibly indulge in low living and do high thinking' (Kellogg 1897[1]:134).

He also set his personal philosophy on the line: 'We want to be health reformers because it is a privilege, and because God has implanted this in our bodies; and he is trying to work to the best ends for us. What a privilege it is to think straight in that way; and if we do it in that way, we will get a blessing in doing it' (*ibid* 136). This is where Kellogg derived his passion – a passion that is more often seen in his earlier writing. This admixture of moral philosophy and physical advice is seen, for example, in Kellogg's book *Social Purity* and in particular in such passages as T*he Effects of Bad Diet* which he describes as the 'road to ruin' (Kellogg 1891:42-56). On other occasions his writings reflect his scientific thoughts and quote from recognised authorities without moral overtones.

A Healthy City

Kellogg was an avid campaigner in every area of health reform. Peter Flynn, a 'Healthy City' protagonist, reminds us that there is a negative side to campaigns: 'Campaigns can actually widen the gap between the health status of groups, where they are predominantly taken up by more affluent people with the income and resources and therefore choices to exploit them and achieve improvements in health and lifestyle' (Flynn 1992:39). He continues, 'Nevertheless there are examples of local projects and policies in every city which empower individuals and groups, and achieve improvements in health. A healthy city is one in which the conditions exist or are being created to allow people to exploit the potential which exists in every individual and location' (*ibid*).

Ninety-six years earlier the *New York Observer* wrote of Kellogg's work in Chicago – which grew out of a free dispensary and bath – listing the objectives of his special home and mission work there:

'1. To furnish a clean, comfortable and cheery home to a large class of poor labouring men in large cities, who have no home or social advantages;

2. To aid the homeless, friendless, discouraged, heart-sick, unemployed men in the hour of their sorest need, and endeavour once more to place them in self-supporting employment;

3. To aid the sick poor with free medical attendance and treatment as needed, both at the mission and through visiting nurses who go as angels of mercy to the garet [sic] and cellar homes of the poor, to bath and dress the sick mother or baby, and render such services as the necessities of each case require;

4. To furnish to labouring men a clean, comfortable bed in a well-ventilated room in summer, and heated in winter at ten cents per night, also free baths, free laundry and a free reading room, gospel meetings, with lectures on health and hygiene;

5. To furnish a lunch of wholesome, well cooked soups, grain foods, and bread and coffee at one cent a dish;

6. To furnish work and training in schools and work shop on the mission farm for the unemployed, many of whom are unable to get work in the cities and who need building up physically before they can be helped morally' (NY Observer 1896:212).

The farm, and also a 'Social Settlement', were already
functioning and well supported. The Social Settlement was
for the use of women and children, with free kindergartens,
kitchens, and mothers' meetings with lectures on health,
cleanliness and religion. The paper reports that hundreds of
mothers and children had used the facility. It also reported
an orphanage belonging to Kellogg located on another farm
of over a hundred acres. The hundred and four orphans
'receiving the most systematic training physically,
intellectually and morally all in smaller groups presided over
by a mother' (*ibid*). Kellogg and his wife adopted fourteen of
these children and fostered a further twenty-eight through
the years. Kellogg was about 44 when this article appeared
in the press. It was his dream that others would take up the
'social settlement' idea. Along with his ideas on sanitary as
well as health reforms, he appears to have anticipated the
'Healthy City' movement by nearly a hundred years.

Race Betterment

Kellogg did not solicit funds for these activities. Apart from
generous donations by interested parties, funding came from
Sanitarium profits, the money generated by his health food
companies, and writing royalties. At a later date the channel
for the projects was another Kellogg creation – the 'American
Medical Missionary Board', further changed to the 'Race
Betterment Foundation'.

This latter-named body was always part of Kellogg's
thinking and touched on his belief that once good health was
fully established it could be passed on from one generation to
another as a genetic inheritance. Kellogg's interest in the
Eugenics movement lay literally in the area of race
betterment. He believed that health reform or biologic living
could upgrade the individual. He further thought it a good
idea to encourage breeding from among those already well
endowed with desirable traits and characteristics of health.
To this end a register of such individuals would be useful.

Kellogg convened three race-betterment conferences in the United States, attracting international attendance. At the Conference held in San Francisco Kellogg raised the matter of the eugenic register acting as a standard, 'Such a registry would be the beginning of a *new* and *glorified* human race, in which societies, far down in the future, will have so mastered the forces of nature that disease and degeneracy will have been eliminated. Hospitals and prisons will have been eliminated. Hospitals and prisons will be no longer needed, and the *golden age* will have been *restored* as the crowning result of human *achievement*, and obedience to biological laws' (Paulson 1916). Kellogg's statement reflects back to the pre-millennial perfectionism of the old-style reformers that he was so anxious to disassociate himself from and not the Adventism that he had followed through the years.

The first World War interfered with the convening of Eugenics conferences, although the attendance and publicity at the three held were good. It is possible that many who attended the conferences had their own views and agendas as to how eugenics might be used for race betterment, and these meetings might have contributed inadvertently to the appalling genocide of later wars, an effect Kellogg would have been among the first to regret. He spoke at the third conference held in the Battle Creek Sanitarium on the now familiar subject of *Habits in Relation to Health and Longevity*. Over sixteen hundred articles reporting the conference appeared in more than five hundred papers in North America, thus continuing to spread this particular aspect of the subject of health reform.

The *Good Health* journal which Kellogg edited for more than seventy-five years became the official organ of the Race Betterment Foundation and survived Kellogg's death by twelve years.

A Hygienic School

One of the practical ways of carrying race betterment or
health reform forward was the establishment of a school for
the purpose. By the turn of the nineteenth century there
were four medical schools in America, and by the twentieth
century America had one hundred and fifty-five medical
schools, only fifty of which were university based (Werbach
1986:16). Werbach comments, 'There was little evidence,
however, that [the university] training produced better
practitioners' (*ibid*). Admission standards for most of the
courses were abysmally low, and the courses were informal
and based on an apprenticeship system which left the quality
of education uneven.

Perhaps remembering the inadequacies of his own training
at Trall's *Hygieo-Therapeutic College* and his subsequent
attendance at *Bellevue*, Kellogg proposed to open a 'Hygienic
School'. In the *Health Reformer* of August 1878, the school
was announced as 'not only the first, but the only school of
the sort in America.' It was not to be a medical school but
rather a health education school, able to provide the kind of
background useful to either health promotion or as a pre-
medical course. In describing its purpose Kellogg wrote:

> 'Only one college in the United States has a
> professorship of hygiene . . . It is to supply this lack,
> only, that this school is to be opened. It is not
> intended in any sense to take the place of a regular
> medical course, but simply to give to individuals
> wishing to commence the study of medicine a basis for
> a broad, liberal, thorough, and practical medical
> education, and to supply to those desiring only a
> limited amount of medical knowledge an opportunity
> to become familiar with a large share of the practical
> knowledge in the hands of the profession, divested of
> its technical dress, simplified, and put in shape to be
> readily utilised' (Kellogg 1877[2]).

Kellogg anticipated that there would be a considerable

number of young people who would not want to become
doctors but who would be interested in health reform. He
encouraged these by stating: 'There are hundreds of our
young men and women who should attend this school.
Sickness is everywhere, and there is no more successful
method of removing prejudice than to be able to enter the
sickroom and relieve the afflicted' (*ibid*). Kellogg hoped that
there might be a hundred lecturers in the field educating the
people on the subjects which are of the most vital importance
to them – those relating to life and health (Robinson
1943:243). The school, closely associated with the Battle
Creek Sanitarium, opened on 14 January 1878 with a student
enrolment of seventy-five which rose quickly to one hundred
and fifty students.

The course was similar in content to a pre-med course,
covering hygiene, anatomy and physiology, chemistry,
physics, and mental philosophy. Clara Strange, in the *Detroit
Free Press*, said, 'Dr John was perhaps the first to urge "the
uplifted thought" as vital to good health. Mental conflicts
and emotional disorders are responsible for too many of our
ills, he would tell those assembled to hear his talks' (Strange
1964:4B). Kellogg's mental philosophy classes must have had
some influence as Dr William Sadler, one of Kellogg's
students, later became renowned as a Christian counsellor
and psychiatrist. The school issued a certificate of study and
proficiency which was accepted by any medical college in the
United States, allowing entrance to a regular medical course.

Later on, fulfilling a need, a medical college known as the
American Medical Missionary College (Robinson 1943:281),
based on property connected with the Chicago Medical
Mission, opened on 3 July 1895. This eventually merged
with the Medical School of the University of Illinois (Schwarz
1970:107).

The Sanitarium also offered a paramedical course
comprising nursing care, massage and the use of therapeutic
electricity, plus instruction in the work of other branches of
the practical medical department. The primary purpose of

this course was to train workers for the Sanitarium. The
original course was for three months which was quickly
extended to six months and then two years. Training was
amortised by two to five years of service to the Sanitarium
(Robinson 1943:245).

A Proliferation of Sanitariums

Kellogg established a number of Sanitariums in America and
played a role in opening sanitariums in many other countries.
By 1901 there were twenty-seven sanitariums and thirty-one
treatment rooms worldwide. He often travelled around the
American sanitariums lecturing and performing surgery. One
of his former patients from Battle Creek, the famous aviator
Glenn Curtiss, offered Kellogg a property in Miami, worth
over a quarter of a million dollars, for one dollar!
Remarking that it was being offered too cheaply, Kellogg
sealed the deal with a ten dollar bill (GH. 1944:13). Other
properties were not so easily secured. The Miami location
became a miniature Battle Creek as Kellogg spent the warmer
winter months there.

Graduates of Kellogg's Hygienic School who went on to
qualify in medicine at various universities often headed these
new institutions. As Kellogg's work was statedly non-
denominational these leaders came from a variety of
backgrounds.

A number of these institutions opened in Europe, not all at
the same time but all based on the principles of biologic
living as promoted by Kellogg. Switzerland, the Scandinavian
countries, and the United Kingdom saw an upsurge in this
type of institution. Other institutions opened in South Africa
and Australia. Often the only connection that these
sanitariums had with Kellogg was the fact that their owners
had at some stage visited Battle Creek and had been
impressed with Kellogg's work. Doctors William and Charles
Mayo credit their friend Kellogg with the idea for their
founding of the now famous Mayo Clinic (Strange 1964:4B).

Sanitarium doctors promoted the same health principle taught by Kellogg. Dr Alfred B. Olsen and his wife M. Ellsworth Olsen, leaders in the Sanitarium at Caterham in Surrey, wrote: 'If one guiding principle be sought for upon which life can be remodelled, we commend the *"Simple Life"*. Get back to nature' (Olsen 1906:21). They wrote in their own book *The School of Health*, 'Hydrotherapy, having proved an especially effective means of such co-operation, naturally occupies a prominent place in this book. Electricity, massage, medical gymnastics, and other agencies of tried worth are also recommended, while great emphasis is laid on fresh air, pure food, and wholesome surroundings generally' (*ibid* 20). Their book records indebtedness to Kellogg.

British physician Gertrude Brown had a wide experience of Kellogg institutions, having served as a nursing assistant in the Basel, Switzerland, Sanitarium, before going to Battle Creek where she rose to become a health educator, often lecturing in J. H. Kellogg's stead, and medical matron. Completing their medical education in Edinburgh, she and her husband opened small institutions of their own, first in Edinburgh, next in Lundin Links, Fife, then Crieff in Perthshire. This latter institution – Roundelwood – is still flourishing, although others which had opened in the UK have long since disappeared. The establishment of the National Health Service forced these private medical institutions to close, although in the present medical climate they might have continued to do well. The same principles of health reform are still an essential part of Roundelwood's health-enhancement programmes.

Despite the fact that the institutions referred to were started on Battle Creek lines, they had no direct link with the Sanitarium. The charitable status of Battle Creek as drawn up with the State of Michigan declared in one of its statutes: 'No funds of the institution can be lawfully sent outside the state to build or support other enterprises of any kind' (Kellogg 1912:25). Aside from this consideration, Kellogg

was also keen to protect Battle Creek's excellent reputation.
He wrote:

> 'The Battle Creek Sanitarium has no branches and is
> not allied to or affiliated with any other institution
> in the world. It stands alone in its work as a
> separate, distinct organisation, having its own
> mission, its own board of management, and
> supported by its own resources.
>
> 'The Battle Creek Sanitarium is the only
> institution which represents in a thorough and up-
> to-date manner the Battle Creek Sanitarium System
> of treatment; in fact, it is the only one which is
> authorised to announce itself to the public as
> employing the Battle Creek Sanitarium System, as
> it is the only institution which is fitted up with the
> necessary laboratory appliances and the trained
> corps of physicians, attendants and nurses which a
> right application of this system requires' (*ibid* 207).

Passing the Message

Kellogg guarded his system with serious intent – all these
measures were to enable lives to be changed in the manner
which he envisaged. Dr Brown tells of a man who came to
Kellogg's office and asked, 'Doctor, how long will it be
before I can return home and do as I used to do?' Wishing
to teach the man a lesson Kellogg replied, 'Never!' The man
could not understand after his remarkable recovery how this
could be. Kellogg continued sternly, 'Sir, you were brought
here dying, and I am sure you must realise the effort that was
made to save your life. You ask me how soon you can go
back and do as you used to do. I hope you will never be that
foolish, because that is what brought you here. If you have
learned how to take care of your body, I think we can let you
go home next week!' (Brown n.d.:92,93).

Kellogg wasted no opportunity to get his message across.
Even his ninety-first birthday proved an opportune time to
right a few wrongs. Kellogg liked to jog and continued to do

so right up to the time of his death. On his birthday he had just returned from his jog when the newspaper reporters arrived. Charles Marentette, Associated Press Staff Writer, recorded the conversation that ensued (Marentette 1943:1):

The Battle Creek Enquirer and News Article

Kellogg 'vowed he'd done pretty well for a "grass eater".

He chuckled when he said it.

'They called me a "grass eater" back when I first started teaching people about biologic living,' he explained. 'All of us, even those who believed as I did, were laughed at. But I guess we showed 'em.'

He was showing 'em right then at 91 years of age, as he trotted back and forth across a backyard cinder footpath for the benefit of news photographers this past summer.

. . . the doctor broke out in a light sweat from his running, said it was a sign of good health, and wanted to know if 'the boys' had their shots. 'Do it again?' he asked. 'Why I can run like this just as long as you have any film.'

[After speaking about exercise and having his rock-hard muscles felt, Kellogg continued]

'You've got to live right,' he went on.

'You boys smoke?' Getting an affirmative nod, the doctor took a step forward and announced, 'It's bad for you.' [He then lectured them] 'You can't smoke and drink alcohol and expect to live a long life . . . I've been teaching that for years, and I know. Had a cat once and gave it just the smallest drop of nicotine and do you know what happened? It died. Works the same on a man, eventually' [Kellogg continued to lecture the newsmen on the effects of a bad diet] (Marentette 1943:1).

Such was Kellogg's devotion to the Sanitarium and the principles of biologic living that when he died, aside from expenses incurred in settling his estate, all the remaining assets were pledged via the Race Betterment Foundation to continue the work. Kellogg made no private bequests but authorised five executors to see that the work went forward (BCEN.1943:1).

The *Good Health* journal was promised to continue and did until 1955. The editors assured the readership that the spirit of Dr Kellogg would continue and, in fact, had a number of his articles to hand ready to print in subsequent issues. The editor stated that 'A few days before the end, by dictating continuously to one of his secretaries for twelve hours without intermission except to take a little food', Kellogg had prepared some excellent articles. During the more than seventy years he had written nearly every word that appeared in the journal – and this at a time when he was editing or contributing to other journals (GH. 1944:4).

Provision was also made for the continuation of the Sanitarium work. More than eighty members of the staff had worked for twenty or more years at the Sanitarium and were devoted to Kellogg and his ideals. Accordingly the Sanitarium 'family', across the whole spectrum of workers, drew up and signed a resolution honouring Kellogg's memory (*ibid*):

Battle Creek Sanitarium Employees' Resolution

'WHEREAS, Dr John Harvey Kellogg devoted to the upbuilding of the Battle Creek Sanitarium the principal efforts of his long and distinguished life;

AND WHEREAS, WE, the active workers in the institution, believe that the finest tribute we can pay to the memory of Dr Kellogg consists in dedicating ourselves to perpetuating the work established by him in accord with his enlightened health principles:

NOW THEREFORE BE IT AND IT IS HEREBY
RESOLVED that the active workers of the Battle Creek
Sanitarium have pledged and hereby do pledge to said
institution as established and carried on by Dr John
Harvey Kellogg our entire and undiminished loyalty,
allegiance and effort, to the end that the Battle Creek
Sanitarium for all time to come shall preserve and
augment its usefulness in accordance with the
principles of its character, and shall continue to afford
to the people of this country and of the world a haven
of health and renewal of the blessings of life' (GH.
1944:4).

Kellogg spent a life in service to the 'San' as it was
affectionately known. One writer, speaking of the role
played by Kellogg's wife Ella and their marriage, said, 'She
played a devoted and efficient second violin in the doctor's
life for over forty years. The first chair was always occupied
by John Harvey's sense of mission to promote the "Gospel of
Health" ' (Johns 1977:51).

Unflagging Zeal

Short in stature, Kellogg made up for nature's deficiency by
using all his energies to promote the principles of health
reform. He was five feet four inches tall and was very
conscious of the fact. To some extent his height acted as a
motivation. One of his secretaries who often saw Kellogg
engaged in posture exercises to enhance his height believed
that he would have liked nothing better than to be six feet
tall (Schwarz 1964:68). Powell described Kellogg as a
'zealot' and a 'dynamo' (Powell 1956:52). Clara Strange
comments of the earlier Battle Creek days that 'The young
doctor pushed, ballyhooed and master-minded an
extraordinary order of health methods at the Sanitarium',
and had, as many others noted, 'incredible drive' (Strange
1964:4B).

Tributes

Over eleven hundred people attended his funeral service and many thousands more heard the service broadcast from Battle Creek radio station which, as an earlier tribute to Kellogg had registered its call sign as W-E-L-L. Tributes came from the famous and the ordinary people of the world who had been touched in some way by his life. The leading newspaper of Battle Creek published a special memorial issue.

Former US Labour Minister, Senator James J. Davis, wrote,

> 'With the passing of Dr John Harvey Kellogg the world has lost an outstanding citizen and mankind a tireless servant. As one who knew the man and followed his work for more than 40 years I am sure that his deep vision, his inventive genius and his driving will to serve will mark him as one of the outstanding men in his field. His was a life rich with service – a life dedicated to the improvement of the science of nutrition and the science of human health' (BCEN 1943:4).

To which remarks may be added from former US President Herbert Hoover: 'Dr Kellogg has lived a long and exceedingly useful life. Many thousands owe their health and happiness to him' (*ibid*).

The church that he had served for a major part of his life, through his scientific underpinning of health reform published two obituaries. The *Review and Herald* summarised his work:

> 'Throughout his entire medical career Doctor Kellogg was a pioneer in the promotion of the principles of health and temperance. He did much in the field of medical research and the development of therapeutic principles and methods. Thousands are indebted to him for the benefits they received from his medical journals, books, lectures, and personal service as a

physician. His death marks the passing of a great man
in the field that he occupied' (RH 1943);

By the time of Kellogg's death the Seventh-day Adventist
Church had a flourishing medical university at Loma Linda,
California. The obituary in their own journal referred to
Kellogg's busy research programme into the causes of
hypertension right up to the day of his death (ME.1944:3).

In delivering his eulogy at Kellogg's funeral, the Revd
Carleton B. Miller, Congregational minister, well summarised
Kellogg's contribution to society:

'For 67 years, John Harvey Kellogg served and saved
his fellowmen here in Battle Creek. Because of his
ministry of healing, many thousands remain to bless
his name and his work in gratitude. There are those
who, having lost health, got it back through him.
There are many more who have been able to keep
their good health and to protect life's greatest prize.

'All over the civilised world people are obeying the
simple, natural truths of biologic living and telling
others of the success of the Battle Creek idea.

'Dr Kellogg sought and found in nature many
answers to life's ailments. In the simple elements of
sunshine, fresh air and exercise he made the weak
become strong. In light, heat and water he restored
the handicapped to usefulness. For foods, he took
grains and cereals, fruits and nuts, finding valuable
minerals and vitamins; and to his discoveries added the
invention of ways to process these foods to make them
attractive to the eye and digestible in the stomach.'

All these would 'bear adequate testimony to Dr
Kellogg's work and achievements' (BCEN 1943:1).

Kellogg would have rejoiced that not only had he managed
to put his message across so that people like Miller could
understand it, but also that all he had tried to do could have
been put so succinctly. To the end Kellogg insisted 'that what
had been accomplished at Battle Creek was not due to his
efforts but was the result of teamwork, and that every person

who had ever been connected with the work had contributed
to the success of the enterprise' (GH.1944:13). This was not
just false modesty on his part. The *Battle Creek Enquirer and
News* comments that a number of people at the Sanitarium had
been part of Kellogg's team for years: Mary Staines Foy having
served sixty-seven years; two others forty-five years each; and
ninety others more than twenty years each. A. F. Bloese served
Kellogg as a private secretary for twenty-eight years. To all
these people Kellogg was not just a leader or a colleague but a
friend. US Senator Arthur H. Vandenbuerg, of Michigan,
might have spoken for them all, 'Dr John Harvey Kellogg was
one of the truly great men of his time – great in his profession
– great in his humanities – great in his citizenship. The world
is better for his having lived, infinitely poorer by his death. We
have all lost a rare benefactor and a precious friend'
(GH.1944:14).

The Road to Wellville

Senator Vandenbuerg's eulogy stands in marked contrast to journalist T. Coraghessan Boyle's parody of the life of Dr Kellogg in his book *The Road to Wellville* (Boyle 1994). Once during his own lifetime Kellogg had been slated by the writer of a pamphlet bearing the same title. The book, however, purports to be the 'greatest story yet: the story of our century, our obsession with healthy living, our terror of mortality'. In the event neither the book nor its screen version starring Sir Anthony Hopkins (*Daily Mail* 1993) made much of an impact, even with its salacious content, except to upset the citizens of Michigan (Laurence 1994).

It would be easy to stand in awe of Kellogg and his considerable achievements. Not all his ideas have stood the test of time but the greater part of his work is acceptable by any recognised standard and he was, for the most part, highly regarded by those who knew him. With the publicity surrounding *The Road to Wellville* book and film his forward thinking should have been open to public scrutiny. Kellogg's work merits serious study rather than the frivolity depicted, and may yet come.

Michael O'Donnell, the editor of the *American Journal of Health Promotion*, defines health promotion as 'the science and art of helping people change their lifestyle to move toward a state of optimal health. Optimal health is defined as a balance of physical, emotional, social, spiritual and intellectual health' (Nieman 1992:123). There can be little doubt in the light of this statement that Dr John Harvey Kellogg made a profound – and probably unsurpassed – contribution to health promotion.

For 'optimal health' read Kellogg's 'biologic living'. Kellogg gave equal weight to physical, emotional, social, spiritual and intellectual health, making a major contribution in each of these vital areas. He appears to have anticipated most of the issues in health promotion today and, even if unacknowledged, his work has contributed to a greater or lesser degree to recognising the problems and suggesting remedies, and will repay close study.

Dr Gertrude Brown posed and answered the question, 'What made Battle Creek so famous throughout the world? Its God-given health principles, its facilities for treatment, a staff of devoted workers, and a combination of spiritual and physical interests' (Brown n.d.:90,91). At its head stood a man totally committed to health promotion – Dr John Harvey Kellogg. Health promotion was not his work – it was his way of life! His concept of 'optimal health' or 'biologic living' was utopian thinking at its very best.

His religion and his way of life – his utopian thinking – was the imperative that pushed his work through to completion. If Kellogg came across as imperious in his manner there could be several reasons. His authority came from absolute conviction. He truly believed that if one adopted the details of his biologic living one would have optimal health and surely be on *The Road to Wellville*. Dr Michael Fitzpatrick notes that in the 1960s Dr Rene Dubos contrasted the two traditions in medicine (depicting them as Hygiea and Asclepius known through classical myth). Dubos stated:

> 'For the worshippers of Hygiea, health is the natural order of things, a positive attribute to which men are entitled if they govern their lives wisely. According to them, the most important function of medicine is to discover and teach the natural laws which will ensure to man a healthy mind in a healthy body.'

On the other hand, Dubos said, stood the followers of Asclepius: 'More sceptical or wiser in the ways of the world', they believe that 'the chief role of the physician is to treat disease, to restore health by correcting any imperfection caused by the accidents of birth or of life' (Fitzpatrick 2001:133). Kellogg's road to Wellville brought both Hygiea and Asclepius together in his visionary Utopia, a task that few others could have accomplished, and set what was to prove an enduring pattern in all that followed in healthful living.

Books by Dr John Harvey Kellogg
As compiled by Richard W. Schwarz

Autointoxication. Battle Creek, 1922.

The Art of Massage: Its Physiological Effects and Therapeutic Application. Battle Creek, 1895.

The Battle Creek Sanitarium Diet List. Battle Creek, 1909.

The Battle Creek Sanitarium System: History, Organization, Methods. Battle Creek, 1908.

The Body in Health. New York, 1915. (With Michael Vincent O'Shea.)

Building Health Habits. New York 1921. (With Michael Vincent O'Shea.)

City Medical Missions. Battle Creek, 1898.

Colon Hygiene. Battle Creek, 1912.

Constipation: How to Fight It. Battle Creek, 1915.

The Crippled Colon: Causes, Consequences, Remedies. Battle Creek, 1931.

Diphtheria; Its Cause, Prevention, and Proper Treatment. Battle Creek, 1879.

Dr. Kellogg's Lectures on Practical Health Topics. 3 Vols. Battle Creek, 1913.

Dyspepsia; Its Causes, Prevention and Cure. Battle Creek, 1879.

The Evils of Fashionable Dress, and How to Dress Healthfully. Battle Creek, 1876.

First Book in Physiology and Hygiene. New York, 1888.

Harmony of Science and the Bible on the Nature of the Soul and the Doctrine of the Resurrection. Battle Creek, 1879.

Health and Cleanliness. New York, 1915. (With Michael Vincent O'Shea.)

Home Hand-book of Domestic Hygiene and Rational Medicine. Rev. ed. Battle Creek, 1900.

Household Manual of Domestic Hygiene, Foods and Drinks, Common Diseases, Accidents and Emergencies, and Useful Hints and Recipes. Battle Creek, 1877.

The Household Monitor of Health. Battle Creek, 1891.

How to Have Good Health Through Biologic Living. Battle Creek, 1932.

How to Save the Babies. Battle Creek, 1916.

Hygiene of Infancy. Battle Creek, 1916.

Ideas. Battle Creek, 1916.

In Memoriam: Ella Eaton Kellogg. Battle Creek (?), ca. 1920. (With H.M. Stegner.)

The Itinerary of a Breakfast. New York, 1920.

Keeping the Body in Health. New York, 1921. (With Michael Vincent O'Shea.)

Ladies' Guide in Health and Disease: Girlhood, Maidenhood, Wifehood, Motherhood. Battle Creek, 1901.

Life, Its Mysteries and Miracles; A Manual of Health Principles. Battle Creek, 1910.

Light Therapeutics; A Practical Manual of Phototherapy for the Student and Practitioner; With Special Reference to the Incandescent Electric-Light Bath. Battle Creek, 1910.

The Living Temple. Battle Creek, 1903.

Making the Most of Life. New York, 1915. (With Michael Vincent O'Shea.)

Man the Masterpiece, or Plain Truths Plainly Told About Boyhood, Youth, and Manhood. Des Moines, Ia., 1886.

Methods of Precision in the Investigation of Disorders of Digestion. Battle Creek, 1893.

The Miracle of Life. Battle Creek, 1904.

The Natural Diet of Man. Battle Creek, 1923.

Neurasthenia; or Nervous Exhaustion with Chapters on Christian Science and Hypnotism, "Habits" and the "Blues". 2nd ed. Battle Creek, 1915.

The New Dietetics; A Guide to Scientific Feeding in Health and Disease. Battle Creek, 1923.

The New Method in Diabetes. 3rd rev. ed. Battle Creek, 1924.

Notes on Practical Hydrotherapy in Use by the Battle Creek Sanitarium and Hospital Training School for Nurses Based upon "Rational Hydrotherapy". Battle Creek, 1919.

Plain Facts About Sexual Life. Battle Creek, 1877.

Plain Facts for Old and Young; Embracing the Natural History and Hygiene of Organic Life. 20th Century ed. Battle Creek, 1901.

The Physical, Moral and Social Effects of Alcoholic Poison as a Beverage and as a Medicine. Battle Creek, 1876.

Practical Manual of Health and Temperance; Embracing the Treatment of Common Diseases, Accidents and Emergencies, the Alcohol and Tobacco Habits, Useful Hints and Recipes. New ed. Battle Creek, 1887.

Proper Diet for Man. Battle Creek, 1874.

Rational Hydrotherapy: A Manual of the Physiologic and Therapeutic Effects of Hydriatic Procedures, and the Technique of Their Application in the Treatment of Disease. Philadelphia, 1901.

Second Book in Physiology and Hygiene. New York, 1894.

Shall We Slay to Eat? Battle Creek, 1899.

The Sinusoidal Current as a Curative Agent; Its History, Technique, and Therapeutic Applications. Battle Creek, 1913.

The Stomach; Its Disorders and How to Cure Them. Battle Creek, 1896.

Sunbeams of Health and Temperance; An Instructive Account of the Health Habits of All Nations. Battle Creek, 1887.

Ten Lectures on Nasal Catarrh; Its Nature, Causes, Prevention, and Cure; and Diseases of the Throat, Eye, and Ear, Due to Nasal Catarrh; With a Chapter of Choice Prescriptions. Battle Creek, 1889.

Text-book of Anatomy, Physiology, and Hygiene; Designed for Use in Colleges, High-schools, Academies, and Families. Battle Creek, 1881.

Tobaccoism, or How Tobacco Kills. Battle Creek, 1922.

A Thousand Health Questions Answered. Battle Creek, 1917.

The Use of Water in Health and Disease; A Practical Treatise on the Bath, Its History and Uses. Battle Creek, 1876.

Why the "Blues", "Nerves", Neuralgias, and Chronic Fatigue or Neurasthenia. 3rd ed. Battle Creek, 1921.

References

ABBOTT, George Knapp; Fred B. Moor; Kathryn L. Jensen-Nelson, (1941), *Physical Therapy in Nursing Care*, Washington: Review and Herald Publishing Association.

Adventist Health, (1982), *National Academy of Sciences Links Cancer to Diet*, Nov/Dec.

ANTROBUS, Derek, (1977), *A Guiltless Feast*, Salford: City of Salford Education & Leisure.

BALL, Bryan W., (1981), *The English Connection*, Cambridge: James Clarke.

Battle Creek Enquirer and News, (1943), Volume XLIX-No. 148, Wed., 15 December.

BLAKE, John B., (1974), *Health Reform*, in *The Rise of Adventism*, GAUSTED, Edwin S., Ed., New York: Harper & Row Publishers.

BOYLE, T. Coraghessan, (1994), *The Road to Wellville*, London: Granta Books.

BROWN, Gertrude, (n.d.), *I Have Lived*, Grantham: Stanborough Press.

COON, Roger, (1993), *The Good Old Days*, Adventist Review, 25 February.

COOPER, Kenneth H., (1970), *The New Aerobics*, Toronto: Bantam Books.

COOPER, Kenneth H., (1989), *Controlling Cholesterol*, Toronto: Bantam Books.

COX, Edward, (1879), *Health Reformer*, Vol. 14, No. 2.

CRAIG, Winston J, (1991), *In the Pink of Health, Adventist Heritage*, Vol. 14, No. 2, Fall Issue.

Daily Mail, (1993), *From serial killer to cereal seller*, 7 May.

DAVIS, Thomas A., (1982), *The National Research Council Says: Reduce Cancer Risk Through Diet, Your Life and Health*, October.

Detroit Free Press, (1964), Sunday, 14 June.

DEUTSCH, Ronald M., (1977), *The New Nuts Among the Berries*, Palo Alto, CA.: Bull Publishing Company.

DOVER, Clare, (1993), *Heart alert on marge, Daily Express,* 5 March.

FITZPATRICK, Michael, (2001), *The Tyranny of Health,* London: Routledge.

FLYNN, Peter, (1992), *Measuring health in cities,* in *Healthy Cities,* ASHTON, John, Ed., Milton Keynes: Open University Press.

GIBBS, Russell, (1979), *Lifestyle and Coronary Heart Disease,* Melbourne: Sun Books.

Good Health, (1944), *A Tribute to a Friend of Mankind,* Vol. 79, No. 1, January.

HALLIDAY, Maddy; Lee Adams, (1992), *Healthy Sheffield, Health Education Journal,* Vol. 51/1.

HANCOCK, Trevor, (1992), *The Healthy City: Utopias and realities, in Healthy Cities,* ASHTON, John, Ed., Milton Keynes: Open University Press.

HARDINGE, Mervyn G., (2001), *Drugs, Herbs & Natural Remedies, Hagerston,* MD.: Review and Herald Publishing Association.

HESSEL, Ted, (1992), *Amazing But True, Guide,* Volume 40, Number 18, 2 May.

HOLLOWAY, Richard, (1999), *Godless Morality,* Edinburgh: Canongate.

JOHNS, Warren L.; Richard H. Utts; Eds., (1977), *The Vision Bold,* Washington D.C.: Review and Herald Publishing Association.

KELLOGG, John Harvey, (1876), *Review & Herald,* Vol. 48, No. 16, 19 October.

KELLOGG, John Harvey, [1] (1877), *Review & Herald,* Vol. 50, No. 25; [2] Health Reformer, June.

KELLOGG, John Harvey, (1878), *Review & Herald,* Vol. 52, No. 16.

KELLOGG, John Harvey, (1879), *Health Reformer,* Vol. 14, January.

*KELLOGG, John Harvey, (1880), *Tobacco Using A Cause of Disease, Good Health*, Vol. 15.

KELLOGG, John Harvey, (1886), Personal letter written to Ellen G. White from battle Creek, dated 12/6/86.

KELLOGG, John Harvey, (1890), *Preface* to *Christian Temperance and Bible Hygiene*, WHITE, Ellen G., Mountain View, California: Pacific Press Publishing Company.

KELLOGG, John Harvey, (1891), *Social Purity*, Battle Creek, Michigan: Good Health Publishing Company.

KELLOGG, John Harvey, (1893), *The Household Monitor of Health*, Battle Creek, Michigan: Good Health Publishing Company.

KELLOGG, John Harvey, (1897), [1] *Health and Spirituality*, General Conference Daily Bulletin, Lincoln, Nebraska, 24 February, Vol. 1, No. 9; [2] *God in Nature*, General Conference Daily Bulletin, Lincoln, Nebraska, 18 February, Vol. 1, No. 5; [3] *Christian Help Work*, General Conference Daily Bulletin, Lincoln, Nebraska, 8 March, Vol. 1, No. 17; [4] *God in Man*, General Conference Daily Bulletin, Lincoln, Nebraska, 22 February, Vol. 1, No. 7.

KELLOGG, John Harvey, (1905), *Medical Missionary*, XIV, March.

KELLOGG, John Harvey, (1912), *Home Book of Modern Medicine*, Vol. 2, London: Henry Camp & Co.

KELLOGG, John Harvey, (1913), *The Battle Creek Sanitarium System*, Battle Creek, Michigan: n.p.

KELLOGG, John Harvey, (1921), *The New Dietetics*, Battle Creek, Michigan: Modern Medicine Publishing Company.

KELLOGG, John Harvey, (1937), *Tobaccoism*, Battle Creek: The Modern Medicine Publishing Co.

KELLOGG, John Harvey, (1938), Script of a talk given at Battle Creek Sanitarium, dated 21 October.

KEZDI, Paul, (1981), *You and Your Heart*, Harmondsworth: Penguin Books.

KOWALSKI, Robert E., (1990), *The 8 Week Cholesterol Cure*, Wellingborough, Northamptonshire: Thorson Publishing Group.

KREUTER, Marshall; Birgitta Hessulf; Donald Maitland; Robert Gould, (1990), *Is cancer on your agenda?*, London: Europe Against Cancer.

KUZMA, Jan W., (1989), *Lifestyle and Life Expectancy of Seventh-day Adventists*, Adventist Review, 29 June.

LAURENCE, Charles, (1994), *Hopkins study of eccentric Kellogg upsets Cereal City, Daily Telegraph*, 27 October, p. 3.

MacKENZIE, Fraser, (n.d.), *How to Avoid Cancer*, London: Skelton Robinson.

MARENTETTE, Charles, (1943), *For 'Grass Eater', Dr Kellogg Reckoned He did Pretty Well*, The Battle Creek Enquirer and News, Vol. XLIX - No. 148, Wednesday, 15 December.

MARVIN, H. M., (1960), *Your Heart: A Handbook for Laymen*, London: Hodder & Stoughton.

Medical Evangelist, (1944), Dr John Harvey Kellogg, Vol. 30, No. 14, 15 January.

MONEY, John, (1985), *The Destroying Angel*, Buffalo, New York: Prometheus Books.

MOZES, Eugene B., (1959), *Living Beyond Your Heart Attack*, Englewood Cliffs, N.J.: Prentice-Hall, Inc.

New Scientist, (2001), *Bathed in light*, 21 July.

New York Observer, (1896), *Dr Kellogg's Work in Chicago*, Vol. LXXIV, No. 32.

NICHOL, Francis D., (1959), *A Nutrition Expert Confirms Ellen G. White Writings*, Review and Herald, 12, 19, 26 February.

NIEMAN, David C., (1992), *The Adventist Healthstyle*, Hagerstown, MD.: Review and Herald Publishing Association.

NOORBERGEN, Rene, (1975), *Programmed to Live*, Mountain View, California: Pacific Press Publishing Association.

NUMBERS, Ronald L., (First published in 1976; a New and Enlarged edition was published in 1992). *Prophetess of Health*, Knoxville: The University of Tennessee Press.

OLSEN, Alfred B.; M. Ellsworth Olsen, (1906), *The School of Health*, London: International Tract Society.

ORNISH, Dean; S. Brown; L. Scherwitz, et al, (1990), *Can lifestyle changes reverse coronary heart disease?*, The Lancet, 336.

PAULSON, David, (1916), Letter in *Paulson Articles and Misc.*, White Estate Document File 269a.

POWELL, Horace B., (1956), *The Original Has This Signature – W. K. Kellogg*, Englewood Cliffs, N.J.: Prentice-Hall, Inc.

REID, George W., (1982), *A Sound of Trumpets*, Washington D.C.: Review & Herald.

Review and Herald, (1943), *Dr J.H. Kellogg*, Vol. 120, No. 52, 30 December.

ROBBINS, John, (2001), *The Food Revolution*, Berkeley, California: Conari Press.

ROBINSON, Dores Eugene, (1943), *The Story of Our Health Message*, Nashville, Tennessee: Southern Publishing Association.

SCHAEFER, Richard A., (1977), *Legacy*, Mountain View, California: Pacific Press Association.

SCHWARZ, Richard W., (1964), *John Harvey Kellogg, M.D.*, Unpublished Doctoral Dissertation, University of Michigan.

SCHWARZ, Richard W, (1970), *John Harvey Kellogg, M.D.*, Nashville, Tennessee: Southern Publishing Association.

SCHWARZ, Richard W, (1990), *Kellogg Snaps, Crackles, and Pops, Spectrum*, Vol. 20, No. 4, June.

SCOTT, Cyril, (1957), *Victory Over Cancer*, London: True Health Publishing Company.

SELYE, Hans, (1974), *Stress Without Distress*, New York: A Signet Book.

Staff, The, (1976), *A Critique of the Book Prophetess of Health*, Washington: The Ellen G. White Estate.

STOLTZ, Garth, (1992), *A Taste of Cereal, Adventist Heritage*, Vol. 15, No. 2, Fall Issue.

STRANGE, Clara, (1964), *The Two Brothers Who Put Michigan on the Map, Detroit Free Press*, Sunday, 14 June.

TANNAHILL, Reay, (1992), *Sex in History*, New York: Scarborough House/Publishers.

THRASH, Agatha; Calvin Thrash, (1981), *Home Remedies*, Seal, Alabama: Thrash Publications.

WALKER, Caroline; Geoffrey Cannon, (1985), *The Food Scandal*, London: Century Publishing.

WALSH, Lynne, (1990), *Take a closer look at a healthy menu*, Health Education News.

WERBACH, Melvyn R., (1986), *Third Line Medicine*, New York: Arkana.

WHITE, Arthur L., (1986), *Ellen G. White, Volume 2, The Progressive Years 1862-1876*, Washington: Review and Herald Publishing Association.

WHITE, Ellen Gould, (1886), Letter to J. H. Kellogg, File No. K64, White Estate.

WHITE, Ellen Gould, (n.d.), *Counsels to Physicians and Medical Students*, (Pamphlet 167), White Estate.

WHORTON, James, (1982), *Crusaders for Fitness*, Princeton: Princeton University Press.

WILLIS, Richard J. B., (1984), *Towards a Theology of Health as it relates to Mission in the Seventh-day Adventist Church*, Unpublished MA Research Paper, Andrews University, Michigan.

WILLIS, Richard J. B., (1993), *The Contribution of Dr John Harvey Kellogg M.D. (1852-1943) to Health Promotion*, Unpublished MSc Dissertation, Brunel University, Middlesex.

WILSON, Michael, (1975), *Health is for People*, London: Darton, Longman & Todd Ltd.

R. A. Williams Library
Florida Hospital College of Health Science
671 Winyah Drive
Orlando, FL 32803